Red Cameras Roll

Direct all Production Inquiries to:
David Lewis
davidcoast@yahoo.com

Red Cameras Roll: The Complete Book and Lyrics of the Musical

Published in the USA by:
BearManor Media
4700 Millenia Blvd.
Suite 175 PMB 90497
Orlando, Florida 32839
www.bearmanormedia.com

Hardcover: ISBN 979-8-88771-150-8
Paperback: ISBN 979-8-88771-149-2

Printed in the United States of America.
Book design by Brian Pearce | Red Jacket Press.

Red Cameras Roll

The Complete Book and Lyrics *of the* Musical

Inspired by the making of
the Bette Davis movie "Storm Center"

MUSIC BY **Max Dancer**

BOOK AND LYRICS BY **David Lewis**

PREFACE

In the summer of 1955, Bette Davis and a film company traveled to the small northern California town of Santa Rosa, to shoot *Storm Center.* The daring venture would come to be considered the first overtly anti-McCarthyism film produced in Hollywood.

In reality, Santa Rosa received the film company with enthusiasm, total cooperation and support. A number of locals landed bit parts in the film or worked as extras. Davis participated warmly in a number of civic events, and was treated well by press and public.

In fact, the film's true theme had been kept a virtual secret. It's working title, *The Librarian,* promised the story of a librarian's relationship to a young boy that had been pitched to the press. *Storm Center's* actual story concerns a book about communism, which the city council presses Alicia Hull, the librarian played by Davis, to remove. She refuses to comply, and is fired. Rumors subsequently circulate about her being a communist, and the young boy who respects her so, suddenly turns against her, and, in the end, sets off a fire in the library. The townspeople come to their senses. Hull is offered her job back, and she vows to sustain her independence in book selection.

There is only one account, in a biography of Bette Davis, of any discord against the movie while it was being made in Santa Rosa. Somebody evidently got wind of the central theme, for a number of women from the Saturday Afternoon Club individually wrote letters to Ms. Davis, urging her to quit the film. She was infuriated, according to the account. But not a word about this made it into the town's one newspaper, the *Santa Rosa Press Democrat.* Not until the film was released, the following year, did the writer and director, Daniel Taradash openly discuss the actual theme.

The movie was met with negative reviews, but in recent years has impressed a growing number of fans, with Davis winning credit her highly controlled, highly believable performance. In 1957, *Storm Center* was awarded the French Prix de Chevalier da la Barre at the Cannes Film Festival, cited as "this year's film which best helps freedom of expression and tolerance."

And what did Bette Davis herself think of the move? She is on record giving good marks for the story, not so good for her young co-star. "I was not overjoyed with the finished film. I had far higher hopes for it. The basic lack was the casting of the boy. He was not a warm, loving type of child. His relationship with the librarian was totally unemotional and therefore robbed the film of its most important factor."

That is debatable. What is not debatable is how totally Davis immersed herself in the role, with not a single trace of the implicit theatrical antics for which she was known and celebrated. From Baby Jane to small town librarian, Alicia Hull — here Bette Davis proved her acting talent to an A.

Red Cameras Roll is totally fictional in its dramatization of a growing public protest against the film, partly fueled by a nasty mayoral election campaign. A secondary plot concerns the romance between Jenny and Bill, two local aspiring actors given bit parts in the film, which is threatened by Jenny's idyllic infatuation with her screen idol, Dayton. Abjectly alone on the set, her personal life in turmoil, Dayton draws closer to Jenny — until idolatry collides with desperation. The character of Jenny was modeld after the Teresa Wright role in another film made in Santa Rosa, Alfred Hitchcock's favorite work, *Shadow of a Doubt.*

CHARACTERS

Scenes have been crafted so that the musical can be performed by a cast of 10-12, with non-principals playing multiple roles.

PRINCIPLES:

BRENDA DAYTON — think Bette Davis in her mid-forties
JOSEPH TOWERS — forty-something, strong, handsome
TED THRALL — late 60s and up, lean, glib, distinguished
ANDY TOMS — early to mid-teens, smart-alecky
MRS. TOMS — 35-40, Andy's good natured mother
JENNY CRANE — early 20's , lovely, dreamy

SECONDARY

appearing in a few scenes

BILL, early 20s, attractively sincere.
STANLEY CHAMBERS, middle aged or up, a blustery politician
GLORIA BAXTER, late 30s, a looker
HEATHER TEMPLE, early 30s, local newspaper reporter

CAMEOS

JUDITH CRANE, mother of Jenny
SIDNEY SLOAN, older Hollywood producer
HEDDA HOPPER, columnist
RUDY ENGLER, blacklisted writer
PROTESTERS
FIREMAN
PARADE ANNOUNCER (*voice only*)
SAM SPARLING, vice mayor

SCENES AND MUSICAL NUMBERS

The time is late summer, 1955

ACT I

SCENE 1: *Outside Union Station, Los Angeles*
Monday morning

MAKING MOVIES — FILM COMPANY
BIGGER THAN LIFE — DAYTON

SCENE 2: *Outside the Rosa Valley train station,*
The following morning

THE COMMUNITY MARCH — SUPPORTERS OF MAYORAL CANDIDATE STANLEY CHAMBERS
AWAY FROM HOLLYWOOD — DAYTON
IN HER MAGIC — JENNY CRANE

SCENE 3: *The living room of the Cranes*
Tuesday, that evening

DUCK AND COVER! — CHAMBERS AND GLORIA

SCENE 4: *Library reading room*
Thursday

MAKING MOVIES — DAYTON AND TOWERS
PUBLIC RELATIONS — DAYTON, TOWERS, AND ANDY

SCENE 5: *Brenda Dayton's hotel suite*
The following Monday

PUBLIC RELATIONS — DAYTON AND HEATHER TEMPLE
THE WRONG PEOPLE LOVE ME — DAYTON

SCENE 6: *Library reading room*
The following Wednesday

MY PARADE — DAYTON

ACT II

SCENE 1: *A small platform, outdoor setting*
The following Saturday

THE COMMUNITY MARCH — A COUPLE OF LOCALS
DUCK AND COVER — ANDY AND MRS. TOMS
MISS TOMORROW — JENNY
IN HER MAGIC — BILL

SCENE 2: *Library reading room*
The following Tuesday

MAKE 'EM SCREAM — ANDY

SCENE 3: *Outside the library*
Thursday

PROTEST SONG — PROTESTERS
DON'T CRY FOR ME, ROSA VALLEY — DAYTON

SCENE 4: *Brenda Dayton's hotel suite*
Saturday evening

PROTEST SONG — PROTESTERS
FALLEN STAR — JENNY
GOODBYE, DEAR FAN — DAYTON
FALLEN STAR — DAYTON

SCENE 5: *Outside the Rosa Valley train station*
Friday morning

MAKING MOVIES — TED THRALL, DAYTON

THE IMAGE OF CAMERAS

During scenes when the company is shooting scenes for the film they are making, the image, if not the reality, of grips working cameras may be suggested in several ways. There could be cameras on the edge of the set or on the extreme edges of the apron. During the shooting of a scene, lights would go on without grips, signifying action. Or the cameras might be "operated" by members of the stage crew, rushing dramatically in each time when called for.

SHOOTING SCENE appears before a scene being shot.

END OF SHOOTING SCENE appears when the shooting ends.

Red Cameras Roll

All lyrics are in **CAPS** *and* **BOLD**

ACT I, SCENE 1: Inside Union Station, Los Angeles, in a roped-off area, suggesting it has been reserved for the film company.

It is Monday morning. TOWERS and SLOAN enter.

ANNOUNCER'S VOICE
ALL ABOARD FOR ROSA VALLEY!
LEAVES IN ONE HOUR!
TRACK NUMBER THIRTEEN!

SLOAN
Where is everyone?

TOWERS
Hiding under the train. Afraid to face reporters.

SLOAN
Reporters? Aren't you leaving town incognito?

TOWERS
Does the press run from controversy?

SLOAN
I'm warning you, Joseph, your bid for respect could backfire.

TOWERS
I'm fronting it, okay?

SLOAN
So, if it's a hit, you're hailed a serious director. You could also be invited to Washington.

TOWERS
If this pushes McCarthy over the edge, maybe just maybe we can…

SLOAN
No No, Joseph! Remember, here's what the public gets fed: a boy's relationship to a librarian.

TOWERS
Mickey Rooney meets Mother Goose?

SONG: "MAKING MOVIES"

SLOAN
MAKING MOVIES SOMETIMES TAKES A DASH OF DECEPTION.
UP IN ROSA VALLEY KEEP THE THEME UNDER COVER.

TOWERS
WHAT ABOUT THE WORLD OF BRENDA DAYTON?

SLOAN
PRAY TO GOD THEY LOVE HER.
WE'RE ON THE BRINK,
HOW ABOUT ANOTHER DRINK?

(TOWERS *and* SLOAN *exit as* MRS. TOMS *and* ANDY *enter*)

MRS. TOMS
They won't make you sing a single song, Andy, I swear.
SIT DOWN, AND THROW THAT GUM AWAY!
ACT LIKE A TROUPER, ANDY.

ANDY
I'M TOO YOUNG,
DAYTON REMINDS ME OF

MRS. TOMS
HOLD YOUR TONGUE!
ANDY, ACT LIKE SOMEONE BIG,
YOU'RE MAKING A MOVIE.

ANDY
ME AND A LIBRARIAN,
NO SHOOTOUTS. NO DEAD GUYS.

MRS. TOMS
BRENDA DAYTON STARS,
AND YOU'RE HER CO-STAR.

ANDY
ME AND OLD MISS RED EYES.

MRS. TOMS
I'LL STRANGLE YOU!

(TOWERS *and* SLOAN *enter, looking around nervously. By now, a few other* CAST MEMBERS *have entered, and the atmosphere becomes more animated*)

SLOAN
YOUR ATTENTION, CAST AND CREW!
(EVERYONE *gives* SLOAN *their attention*)
DON'T LET THE THEME OUT TO THE PRESS.
WE STRESS HOW LITERATURE CAN ELEVATE.

ANDY
(*mockingly, taking his mother's arm*)
BOY HELPS LIBRARIAN LAND A DATE.

SLOAN
(*to* ANDY)
TALK LIKE THAT TO HEDDA HOPPER,
DAYTON MAY KILL YOU.

TOWERS
(*to* SLOAN)
NEED MORE EXTRAS, SYDNEY.

SLOAN
MARTY SCREAMED, "KEEP THE NUT DOWN."
WARNING YOU, IF YOU GO OVER BUDGET,
ROSENBERG WILL SHUT DOWN.
ARE YOU PREPARED?
THIS IS ART, THEY'RE RUNNING SCARED
DAYTON BEHAVES.

TOWERS
HUMBLED NOW, SHE WOULDN'T DARE...

SLOAN

STICK TO THE PLAN,
TIP TOE TILL IT'S IN THE CAN.

(*sees someone approaching*)

Oh, no, there comes Hedda.

TOWERS

Hedda who hates the script. What is she doing here, the two-faced vulture.

SLOAN

Oh, Spying, I suppose, for the House on un-American activities.

(*enter the illustrious* HEDDA HOPPER)

HOPPER

Hollywood to America!
THIS IS HEDDA HOPPER WITH A FILM LAND EXCLUSIVE...
DATELINE: UNION STATION,
THE RETURN OF A LEGEND!
NO ONE'S MOVEMENTS ARE MORE CELEBRATED.

ANDY

(*aside*)

OR MORE CONSTIPATED.

HOPPER

(*recognizing* ANDY)

THAT FACE I KNOW.

MRS. TOMS

ANDY TOMS, MY SON.

ANDY

(*to* HOPPER, *with class*)

HELLO.

SLOAN

(*to* TOWERS)

SHUT THAT LITTLE MONSTER UP.

HOPPER

(*into her mike*)

YOU'VE SEEN HIM ON TV.

ANDY

HERE'S A SCOOP...

(HE *whispers something into* HOPPER'S *ear, and* HEDDA, *puts her mike aside, resolved to spare America from such candor as she is now witnessing*)

SLOAN

(*to* TOWERS)

OH, GOD, WHAT NOW?

TOWERS

(*to* SLOAN)

THE MOTHER'S A NUT CASE.

HOPPER

(*to* ANDY)

WHO TOLD YOU SHE HAD ANOTHER...

(SHE *whispers something into* ANDY'S *ear*)

ANDY

OLD LOUELLA BUTT FACE.

(*aghast,* HOPPER *shuts her mike off, and puts it aside, yet visibly amused by* ANDY'S *slur*)

SLOAN

OH, WHAT A CROCK.

ANNOUNCER'S VOICE

ALL ABOARD AT TEN O'CLOCK!

HOPPER

(*approaching* TOWERS)

ABOUT YOUR CONTROVERSIAL THEME?

TOWERS

SUBVERSIVE LIES, MISS HOPPER
YOU'VE BEEN CONNED.

ANDY

(*wiggling up to* HOPPER, PR *style*)

BOY AND LIBRARIAN FORM A BOND.

ANNOUNCER'S VOICE

ALL ABOARD FOR ROSA VALLEY!
FILM CREW — CAR THIRTEEN!

ANDY

PARLOR CAR FOR MAIDS AND MUMMIES

SLOAN

(*to* TOWERS)

MUZZLE THE MONSTER

HOPPER

(*having turned her mike back on*)

WORLD, THE ROAR OF DAYTON FANS IS NUMBING,
WORLD, SHE'LL SOON BE COMING!

And. while we wait...Here's Joseph Towers!

(SHE *puts her mike in* TOWERS' *face*)

...director of the wartime classic, *On the Shores of Hope*...Tell us, Joseph, how it feels to be directing a more intimate small-town story.

TOWERS

Hedda, thank you! It's a big scary challenge, and I can take it on because we believe there is a place for real human drama without guns going off in every other scene.

HOPPER

Serious human drama. World, are you ready?

(SHE *moves her mike to* ANDY)

Our handsome young new costar on the scene — just off the set of TV's hot...

(SHE *falters for the name.* MRS. TOMS *steps in*)

MRS. TOMS
Teenage Times.

HOPPER
Teenage Times, yes! Andy Toms, how does it feel to be working with Screenland's virtuoso vixen, Brenda Dayton?

ANDY
(*faking sincerity*)
Real fine, Miss Hopper, real fine. I'm thinking I'll learn a lot about acting from the virtuoso vixen. And, so, I've been up nights, ail excited for the golden chance to grow in her shadows.

HOPPER
Isn't he smart! Isn't he wise!
(*spotting someone*)
Could it be...
WORLD, THE FLAMES OF HOLLYWOOD ARE BURNING
DAYTON IS RETURNING

(*enter* BRENDA DAYTON, *in full command*)

DAYTON
(*looking around*)
STILL ON MY FEET,
(*crossing to* HOPPER)
HEDDA, YOU DON'T MISS A BEAT.

HOPPER
HOLLYWOOD YEARNS,
CHEERS ABOUND. A STAR RETURNS!

DAYTON
GOODNESS IMPLORES:
IF I SHINE, MY LIGHT IS YOURS.
(*some cheers from those around*)

HOPPER
World, on my solemn word you have it, she is back. They had written her off. They underestimated her reigning legacy…the indestructible aura… the redoubtable resilience…the…

DAYTON
(*interrupting*)
Oh, Hedda, please!
(HOPPER *puts her mike aside.* DAYTON *turns to* ANDY)
Andy, you'll get over it. There are a million Marilyn Monroes out there. But there is only one…
(*to* TOWERS)
Joseph, darling, great to see you.
(SHE *throws* TOWERS *a kiss, though he is not that far from her.* TOWERS *crosses to take* DAYTON'S *hand,* PR *style*)

ANDY
(*to himself*)
Yuck.

MRS. TOMS
(*to* ANDY)
Shhhh!

HOPPER
Still vibrant. Ever tenacious!

DAYTON
If you can hold on, so can I.

HOPPER
(*with her mike back in use*)
Tell our millions of listeners, Brenda: from your many roles, wayward woman to doomed diva, how will it feel pushing a date stamp at the check-out counter?

DAYTON
The date stamp is only a prop, dear Hedda. As you well know, I have always been an avid reader. Hemingway. Wharton, *The New Yorker.* I

am going to make all librarians who suffer the prissy stereotype proud to be who they are.

HOPPER
Tell our listeners, please, Brenda, the key to your legendary success?

SONG: "BIGGER THAN LIFE"

DAYTON
THIS MUCH I KNOW:
THEY'RE GONNA GET ME.
I GO FOR BROKE IN EVERY ROLE.
GODDESS OR TRAMP —
I'M BIGGER THAN LIFE,
THAT'S MY GOAL.

TO KEEP A CROWD
ENSLAVED IN THE DARK,
I DRAW THEIR SCORN,
I MAKE 'EM SOB.
GIVE THEM EMOTIONS BIGGER THAN LIFE —
THAT'S MY JOB.

IN ALL ITS WONDER,
ACTING IS LIFE.
I WAKE UP EVERY DAY TO CREATE
THE GREAT ILLUSIONS THAT WE LIVE FOR.
MAKING MAKE BELIEVE WORK IS MY FATE.

THIS MUCH I KNOW,
AWARDED, OR SNUBBED,
DOWN IN THE DUMPS
ABOUT TO CRACK.
COME FAME OR SHAME,
I'M BIGGER THAN LIFE,
SMEAR MY NAME
SACK ME JACK
I'M STILL BACK!

HOPPER
And she's back, alright!

(HOPPER *is distracted by* ANDY *and* MRS. TOMS, *trying to snare her attention. towers, aware of* DAYTON'S *ego, stays placatingly to her side*)

DAYTON
Here's a scoop for the world of Hopper.

TOWERS
(*to* DAYTON *privately*)
Remember what we don't reveal.

DAYTON
(*appearing to charge ahead, to* HOPPER)
Gish, Harlow, Turner, Gardner…who else…Betty Boop, they all said no to this role. Then they came to me…
(*a hush.* EVERYONE *looks riveted*)
…out of desperation. And I signed on out of courage. I think it's an important film. I don't work just for money. I work to work. I act to act. I am because I am!
(SHE *sings.*)
IT FEELS LIKE MAGIC TO BE HERE,
TO BE EMBARKING ON ANOTHER SHOOT.

HOPPER
HOW DO YOU STAY SO YOUNG?

DAYTON
NUTS AND FRUIT.
MAKING MOVIES, YOU'RE ON TOP WHENEVER YOU START OUT.
(*pause*)
Well, everybody. Are you?

A FEW OTHERS
MAKING MOVIES: PRAY TO GOD THEY WON'T TEAR YOUR PART OUT.

AND YET MORE
PEOPLE WHO CAN'T MAKE IT IN OHIO.
OUT HERE MAKE A BIO.

MOST OF THEM
EXTRAS BEWARE: MAKING MOVIES ISN'T FAIR.
WE FAKE MAKING MOVIES WHEN THE PUBLIC IS WATCHING.
ORCHESTRATED CHAOS GIVES 'EM DRAMA AND COLOR.
RARELY ARE THE CAMERAS EVER ROLLING.
NOTHING COULD BE DULLER, IN BETWEEN TAKES.
KISSING UP TO GRIPS AND FLAKES.

DAYTON, HOPPER AND ANDY
STILL IT'S AMAZING HOW IT WORKS,
AND HOW IT FEELS APPEARING IN A SCENE,
SEEING YOURSELF UP THERE ON THE SCREEN.

MOST OF THEM
MAKING MOVIES ACTUALLY IS VERY DEPRESSING.
MOST OF US GET MINIMUM,
NO THANKS AND NO BILLING.
STILL WE WOULDN'T TRADE IT FOR A DAY JOB.
HOLLYWOOD, WE'RE WILLING!

WOMAN
STOOD IN FOR JACK,
CAPRA SAID HE'LL CALL ME BACK!

MAN
MET DORIS DAY,
ASKED ME FOR MY RESUME!

MRS. TOMS
I GOT A LINE:
LASSIE BARKS, I SAY "I'M FINE."

DAYTON
WARNING MY DEARS:
FAME IS NOT WHAT IT APPEARS.

HOPPER
Fame is not what it appears, world, says Brenda Dayton.

DAYTON
MAKING MOVIES OUGHT TO BE AS DARING AS LIFE IS.
MAKING MOVIES OUGHT TO SHINE A LIGHT IN THE DARKNESS
ME, I FIGHT FOR SCRIPTS THAT I BELIEVE IN,
IN OR OUT OF FASHION

(*The insistent blow of a train whistle*)

DREAMERS, WE FLY
EVERY FILM, ANOTHER TRY

ANNOUNCER'S VOICE
All aboard, North Coast Central!

(*The* CAST *and* CREW *hurry off through a door to the tracks as the train whistle blows again*)

DAYTON
WAIT FOR ME TRAIN...
HOLD YOUR STEAM, I'M COMING TOO!

Optional Transition "Movietone" Sequence

A scrim may rise to conceal the set, and on it would be projected Movietone type images — shots of the cast and crew en route to Rosa Valley, while we hear:

MOVIETONE ANNOUNCER'S VOICE
Hollywood film crews with legendary Brenda Dayton on board, training up to Rosa Valley for on-site shooting of *My World of Books.* Hedda Hopper probing strange secrecy on the set and predicting a box office bonanza for Dayton's new movie, a card catalogue expose with controversy stamped all over it. Fans already lining up at the check-out counter for a glimpse of the famed actress in her latest comeback!

(*"Movietone" musical background fades out*)

ACT I, SCENE 2: The next morning, outside the much smaller Rosa Valley train station.

JENNY stands alone, acting out a day dream.

JENNY

(*to an imaginary audience*)

Thank you, thank you, Hollywood, for making this the greatest moment of my life, and to my mother and father, for their belief in my dreams! I shall forever cherish this trophy, world!

(BILL *enters, applauding*)

BILL

Bravo to a new star! I can't wait for the filming to begin.

JENNY

Can you believe it, Bill, both of us getting to appear in the picture! Aren't you glad I pushed you to auditions?

BILL

Yes, I am, but you have three words more than I do, Marlene.

JENNY

Sorry about that, Edward.

(JENNY *giggles,* BILL *gives her a hug*)

Listen, Jenny. After school, Mr. Bower coached me for a whole hour on how to deliver the line they sent me.

JENNY

He did?

BILL

He got me to dig deeper, to draw from my own experience, something they teach you in New York. It was soul expanding.

JENNY

It was? Well, let me hear the line now, Bill.

BILL

(*taking a few moments to get into the part*)

Thank you Miss Lake, I'll read it.

JENNY

Yes, Bill. Now I can feel it deep inside you. In fact, I see Brando.

BILL

Brando? Maybe in the sub text?....

JENNY

Sub text, yes, Bill. It makes you sound so professional. We may start out as extras, but once they see us in action, we are going to be more than extras.

BILL

(*hugging* JENNY)

Do you have your line memorized?

JENNY

(*thinks, goes into a part and recites*)

I am, Miss Lake! My mother thinks I'll be a teacher.

BILL

Wait till they hear you.

(*We hear singing voices in the distance, and then* CHAMBERS SUPPORTERS *enter*)

SONG: "THE COMMUNITY MARCH"

CHAMBERS SUPPORTERS

VOTE FOR STAN!
HE'S THE MAN!

HE'S THE MAN WHO'LL KEEP US TRUE
TO THE RED WHITE AND BLUE
VIRTUES OF THE FREE.
ROSA VALLEY MAYOR TO BE!

NEVER WEAK!
NEVER RED!
NEVER GLIB WITH LIBERTY!
STANLEY CHAMBERS FOR STRONG
CITIZENS ON CALL
AND FOR FALLOUT SHELTERS FOR ALL!

VOTE FOR STAN!
STAN WHO CAN
LIFT THE LID ON CITY HALL,
SUBVERSIVES EXPOSED
AND SENT ON THE RUN.
NO VACATIONS FOR STAN,
WON'T BE DONE TILL HE'S DONE!

VOTE FOR STAN
HE'S THE MAN!

(THEY *march off, music fades away*)

JENNY

(*sensing* BILL'S *excitement*)

Are you voting for him, Bill?

BILL

Not sure, but he makes a lot of sense, and why should I vote for a mayor who puts big game hunting over his own reelection.

JENNY

Seem's odd to me too. I don't know. The train should be here any moment. The way they have it roped off back there, must be expecting a big crowd, but where are the people?

BILL

Brenda Dayton is not that big a star anymore.

JENNY

(*strangely preoccupied*)

Oh, but she will be, Bill, again.

(*A train whistle*)

JENNY
It's coming! She is the queen of comeback. To think, any moment now, she will be stepping through that door, and across the grass, and breathing the air we breathe.

BILL
Well, don't get carried away, Jenny.

JENNY
Oh, but I have to. I'm her number one fan. We're like sisters, almost.

BILL
(HE *places a kiss on* JENNY'S *forehead*)
After our big break, maybe then, Jenny, do you suppose we can, ah, do what we've been planning on.

JENNY
(*evasively, pulling away, as the train arrives*)
I'm so nervous, Bill, I feel as if I've known her all my life and she is finally coming back for a long overdue visit.

(*The doors open, and through them come a modest number of film company members.* JENNY *stands slightly at a poetic distance, as if not wishing to encroach on a dream.* TED THRALL, MRS. TOMS, ANDY, *and* JOSEPH TOWERS *enter, followed by a few others.*

Finally, BRENDA DAYTON *enters, and the few onlookers on the scene join* JENNY *and* BILL *in offering a modest cheer. Remarkably,* DAYTON *plays up their attention to the hilt, as if she is moving through a large crowd of fans at a Grauman's Chinese Theatre premier.*)

SONG: "AWAY FROM HOLLYWOOD"

DAYTON
WELL, HELLO THERE, FOLKS!
HEY, IT'S GREAT TO BE ON LOCATION HERE.
IF I SHED A TEAR,
GO AHEAD AND ASK, WHY I'M FEELING SO GOOD.
I'M AWAY FROM HOLLYWOOD!

I CAN WALK TO TOWN,
SAY, "HELLO! HELLO!"
EVERY FACE I SEE LOOKS FRIENDLY TO ME.
SOMEONE, TAKE MY HAND.

(JENNY *extends a hand, but too far from* DAYTON *for the latter to notice.*)

SOMEONE, STRIKE UP THE BAND.
I'M AWAY FROM LA LA LAND!
I'VE BEEN TOO LONG WHERE PEOPLE ARE CARDBOARD.
FOR A PENNY, ANYTHING GOES.
DOWN IN TINSEL TOWN, HAPPINESS IS
YOUR CHOICE OF GIGOLOS.

ISN'T GLITZ THE PITS?
GIVE ME REAL LIFE.
BREAKFAST ON A TRAY AT WOOLWORTH'S CAFÉ.
I WILL WAIT MY TURN
LIKE A GOOD NEIGHBOR SHOULD.
IF I UTTER,
"DAMN YOU, WAITRESS! WHERE'S THE BUTTER?"
PARDON ME, I'M FROM HOLLYWOOD!

(*Some cheers from the small crowd. The finely attired* SPARLING *enters*)

SPARLING
Miss Dayton: on behalf of our Mayor Duncan, who is away at the moment, it is my honor to extend his warmest official wishes to you and your film company on your time in Rosa Valley.

DAYTON
Well thank you…And you're?

SPARLING
I'm Sam Sparling, the vice mayor.

DAYTON
How nice!

FAINT VOICE IN THE CROWD
Chambers for mayor!

(DAYTON *is a bit startled, and then makes brief eye contact with* JENNY *as* HEATHER TEMPLE, *local columnist, edges up to* DAYTON *with pencil and paper in hand*)

TEMPLE
Miss Dayton: For the *Rosa Valley Register,* could you tell us a little about "My World of Books."

DAYTON
Oh, what can I tell you. Well. I face one of the most challenging acting jobs I have ever been handed, to play a librarian who nurtures young readers, in particular, a troubled teenager who could go either way in life.

(SHE *looks around*)

...Andy, where are you?

(MRS. TOMS *pushes* ANDY *up to* DAYTON. DAYTON *wraps her arm around* ANDY, *who looks uncomfortable*)

A marvelous young face off the TV circuit. And had they not canceled his show, he would not be gracing our company.

TEMPLE
(*To the rather unimpressed* ANDY)

Well, how lucky we are to have you in our midst!

ANDY
Yeah, you are. And my show wasn't canceled.

TEMPLE
It wasn't?

ANDY
I got bored, and quit.

TEMPLE
Well, I hope you enjoy making movies, Andy!

(HE *makes an exaggerated smile.* TEMPLE *turns to* DAYTON)

TEMPLE
And what made the film company chose Rosa Valley?

DAYTON
We wanted an idyllic American town, and how idyllic it feels to be here. Even the faces in the crowd, I am reminded of my own early innocence, and how I wish I were back there.

(*focusing on* JENNY)

I know that some of you in Rosa Valley have been cast to play parts in the film. Others may yet be. And in your eager faces, I see my own youthful dreams.

TEMPLE
I almost forgot, Miss Dayton. My newspaper, which sponsors the event, is hoping that you will agree to be a guest judge at Nancy Bell's Annual Talent Roundup.

DAYTON
It should be wonderful. I gratefully accept! And may I invite my dear colleague, veteran hoofer Ted Thrall, to join us in some fashion?

TEMPLE
Oh, indeed, you may!

THRALL
A talent show. Very, very bright. Eager young thespians and hoofers… troubadours up and coming, fresh comics! Beautiful babes and ever humming…

DAYTON

(*as an aside, feeling upstaged*)

Oh, yes Ted!

THRALL
I am humbly flattered.

(THRALL *wins instant vigorous applause,* HE *is so immediately ingratiating*)

DAYTON

(*wanting the spotlight back on herself*)

I'M AWAY FROM JACK'S IMBECILIC CRACKS,
HEDDA HOPPER'S GLARE,
MONROE OVER AIR,
LIBERACE'S HOSE,
ROSE VALLEY, YOU'RE ON.
LEAD ME OUT OF BABYLON!

FREE FROM MONSTER TYKES,
TEMPLE LOOK-ALIKES,
BODY BUILDING CLODS,
EGYPTIAN FACADES.
MAKE ME SCREAM FOR LOVE
FROM A PARK BENCH ALONE,
FAR AWAY FROM MOVIETONE.

OTHERS

SHE'S HAD HER FILL OF SILVER SCREEN ROMANCE.
THOSE WITH NO CHANCE RAVISH HER...

DAYTON

BUT...
EVERY TIME I FALL MADLY IN LOVE,
SOME JOKER HOLLERS "CUT!"
CUT THE BALLYHOO.
TURN THE WORLD BACK ON
TO A SMOGLESS SKY,
THE SCENT OF A COW,
SACRED GRASS THAT GROWS.
ROSA VALLEY, BE GOOD.
KEEP ME FAR FROM TORRID TINSEL,
EMPTY STARDOM.
HELP ME SOME, I'M FROM HOLLYWOOD!

(*Despite* HER *people oriented sentiments,* DAYTON *rushes off, presumably to a waiting automobile or limousine.* JENNY *looks hurt and perplexed*)

JENNY
(*to* BILL)
She said she would walk to town. In a Cadillac?

BILL
That was just a song, Jenny, from "Main Street Rhythm."

JENNY
But it wasn't a Dayton movie. Anyway, she'll walk to town with me. We read each other's minds perfectly.

BILL
What do you say about us walking to town for something to eat?

JENNY
Oh, not yet, Bill. I can't.

BILL
We made a date, Jenny. Remember?

JENNY
Did we.

BILL
I offered you a sandwich and soda at Mac's.

JENNY
Yes, you did, and I'm not trying to put you off.

BILL
Is something wrong?

JENNY
Oh, no, but can I take a rain check, Bill? I have to stay here for a spell and savor it all. So much has happened, Bill. She called our grass sacred, I want to memorize every detail of our first meeting. You will understand?

(*some laughter from* OTHERS, *entertained in the background by* THRALL *and* ANDY)

BILL

(*turning to leave*)

Then…I guess I'll see you later?

JENNY

(*faintly, lost in her day dreaming*)

You will, Bill.

BILL

I'll…

(*Sensing the futility in trying to communicate, dejected and confused,* BILL *exits*)

SONG: "IN HER MAGIC"

JENNY

I'LL WRAP MYSELF IN HER MAGIC
AND SAVE EVERY SCENE WE SHARE.
I'LL MEMORIZE HOW SHE SMILED
THE MOMENT I SAW HER THERE.
THE DAWNING GLOW OF A FRIENDSHIP,
DID SHE FEEL THE SAME? SHE MUST.
BUT IF I'M BLINDED BY STARDUST,
SWEET FANTASY, I'M YOUR SLAVE.
ONE MORE TAKE, PLEASE,
HEART, DON'T BREAK, PLEASE.

I'LL BE BRAVE.
LET THE CAMERAS ROLL
FOR ME AND MY BRIGHT SHINING STAR.
FOR HER LOVE OR FOR DREAMS CRASHING DOWN,
I'LL FOLLOW HER ANYWHERE.
I'LL WRAP MYSELF IN HER MAGIC.
WHENEVER I WISH, I'LL SEE
SAME RISING SMILE WHEN SHE ENTERS,
SAME SETTING, SAME LIGHT, SAME AIR.
ONE MORE TAKE, PLEASE.
HEART, DON'T WAKE, PLEASE.

(*The focus shifts to* TOWERS, THRALL, *and* MRS. TOMS *in a downstage crossover*)

THRALL
SHE'S FREE FROM ALL HER CORNY ILLUSIONS.

MRS. TOMS
MOTION PICTURES AREN'T WHAT THEY WERE.

THRALL AND TOWERS
FREE FROM ALL OF HER SUITORS WHO SUIT
EACH OTHER MORE THAN HER.
SHE CAN WALK TO TOWN,

MRS. TOMS
(*mimicking the Great One*)
SAY "HELLO! HELLO!"
EVERY FACE I SEE LOOKS FRIENDLY TO ME.
CHAT WITH AVERAGE FOLKS.
HOPE IT'S WELL UNDERSTOOD
IF WE CAN'T BE SYMBIOTIC, I'M PSYCHOTIC
WORSHIP ME. I'M FROM HOLLYWOOD.

ACT I, SCENE 3: The living room of the Crane home. It can be as simply furnished as need be, or suggested by minimal props.

The same day. Present are CHAMBERS, MRS. CRANE, GLORIA, and, optionally, a few WOMEN seated on single chairs.

MRS. CRANE

(*addressing the group, and by extension, the audience*)

Ladies of light, our special guest this afternoon — candidate for mayor of Rosa Valley, Stanley Chambers!

(*Polite applause as* CHAMBERS *rises, feigning humility in a hackneyed manner*)

CHAMBERS

Thank you. Thank you, Mrs. Crane and Ladies of light. I praise your civic devotion, your vigilance on Skywatch atop the courthouse roof. Your spirit will be the cornerstone of my mayoral campaign!

(*vigorous applause.* HE *turns mawkishly sentimental*)

I vow to protect our freedom from godless tyranny by purging all subversive elements out of this community!

(*applause*)

About the movie being filmed in our midst, I was cheered to learn of a letter you have written to Brenda Dayton, at the hotel where she is now staying, urging her to rethink her commitment to this film and walk away from it.

(*cheers*)

Yes, I agree! To you, ladies of light, I pledge a total integrity overall at city hall if elected your next mayor!

(*Some cheers, big applause*)

On a lighter note, I've learned of your duck and cover song for the school kids, composed, I understand, by several among you…

(HE *winks at* GLORIA)

…and, well, I was charmed by the ditty, all the way onto my feet! Can you imagine that?

(*laughter*)

I'm not much of a dancer, but…

GLORIA
Stanley would love to use it in his campaign.
(*vigorous applause*)

CHAMBERS
(*to* GLORIA)
But I don't tap! Should we give them a little preview, Gloria?

(*Laughter and encouraging cheers from those in attendance.* GLORIA *joins* CHAMBERS)

SONG: "DUCK AND COVER"

CHAMBERS
ONE DAY AT SCHOOL YOU HEAR

GLORIA
JETS ROAR.
THE CEILING SHAKES, BUT YOU

CHAMBERS
STAY CALM.
YOUR CLASSMATES ALL SHOULD BE

GLORIA
INSIDE.
AND IF THEY AREN'T, YOU YELL

CHAMBERS AND GLORIA
H BOMB!

GET DOWN,
DO THE DUCK AND COVER!
GET DOWN,
HIT THE FLOOR AND HOVER.
FOLLOW THIS RULE, YOU'LL BE
RADIOACTIVE FREE.

CHAMBERS
BOMBS BURST,

GLORIA
DO THE DUCK AND COVER.

CHAMBERS
HEAD FIRST,

GLORIA
COVER UP FOR FREEDOM.

CHAMBERS AND GLORIA
WINNING THE WAR FOR IKE,
COMMIES, GO TAKE A HIKE!

WOMAN
SAY I'M IN THE JOHN,
BUT I'M NOT DONE YET?

GLORIA
DO IT ON THE RUN INSTEAD

CHAMBERS
RUN FOR COVER FIRST.
DEPOSIT LATER

CHAMBERS AND GLORIA
BETTER TO BE WET THAN TO BE DRY AND DEAD.
GET DOWN,
EVERY GIRL AND BOY GET GOING.
JOHNNY, OFF THE TOILET!
COVER YOUR HEAD TO TOES
HOVER AND HOLD YOUR NOSE

MRS. CRANE
UNDERNEATH A TREE, A COW, A DUMP TRUCK.

WOMAN
UP TO HERE IN MUD AND POOP.

CHAMBERS AND GLORIA

DO THE DUCK WITH ME,
I'LL BE YOUR COVER
UNDERNEATH YOUR BED, OR IN MY CHICKEN COUP.

(*Optionally, some of the* LADIES *may join in, and whoop it up in wild dancing abandon, in which case they are alternately on their feet and on the floor mimicking "duck and cover" positions*)

MOST OF THEM

GET DOWN.
DO THE DUCK AND COVER!
LAY LOW
LOW AS ANY SNAKE GOES
HIDING IN DUNG AND DIRT.
DOING THE RED READ ALERT!

ACT I, SCENE 4: Open area at the Rosa Valley library. A check out desk, a few reading tables, some shelves containing books.

Thursday, two days following. DAYTON is seated at the check-out desk. BILL playing Edward is seated at a reading table. ANDY, playing Rusty, enters with a book in hand.

SHOOTING SCENE

ANDY

(*playing Rusty, who fakes being a goody-good around adults*)

Good morning, Miss Lake, and how well-combed you look.

DAYTON

And how well preserved you make me feel, Rusty.

ANDY

I hope your date stamp is as fresh with ink as are your shelves with new books.

(HE *hands the book to* DAYTON)

DAYTON

(*impressed by his selection*)

Well, well, Rusty, I see you have one. *Russia Today.* You are traveling far, and I applaud your open-mindedness.

ANDY

I have found that some of the best books are on the higher shelves.

DAYTON

And only a few steps up the foot ladder.

(SHE *stamps the book out and hands it to* ANDY. *as* JENNY, *playing Marlene, enters, with a book in hand*)

I hope you learn a lot. Oh, Rusty!...

(SHE *hands him a book*)

Will you please give this book to Edward over there.

(BILL *looks up, as* ANDY *approaches him*)

I found something on geology that you might like, Bill

BILL (*as Edward*)
Oh, thank you, Miss Lake! I'll read it.

(ANDY *exits*)

DAYTON
And how nice to see you, Marlene. You are fond of history.

JENNY (*as Marlene*)
I am, Miss Lake! My mother thinks I'll be a teacher.

DAYTON
And a very good one at that.

JENNY
I hope so!

END OF SHOOTING SCENE

TOWERS
Cut!
(*to* JENNY *and* BILL)
You both did wonderfully. And in only two takes! You show a natural gift for this.

JENNY AND BILL
Oh, thank you, Mr. towers.

TOWERS
Alright, your work is over for the day. And, if there are any more scenes we need you for, we'll be in touch.

JENNY AND BILL
(*leaving*)
Thank you!
(THEY *exit*)

TOWERS
Okay, let's continue where we left off. Camera, lights, action!

SHOOTING SCENE

(THRALL, *playing Hank, enters*)

DAYTON
How early to see you, Hank, at this time of the day.

THRALL (*as Hank*)
The sun is out!

DAYTON
Something is on your mind. Now who's rattling it?

THRALL
Somebody was complaining about one of your new books…

DAYTON
Not mine, Hank. Ours.

THRALL
The subject is…

DAYTON
Oh, yes, that one.

THRALL
It's starting to become an issue.

DAYTON
I could have predicted.

THRALL
Really, Harriet. You already have a few on the subject.

DAYTON
And one of them was checked out by one of our brightest boys

THRALL
A boy? This is hardly a book for…

DAYTON
For a young mind? Rusty is a most…

THRALL
What, Harriet? Please. This could become a thorny issue at the mayor's office, and they may ask you to take it down or at least keep it in limbo until the election.

DAYTON
I do not keep books in limbo, Hank, while politicians compete for patriotism awards. A true library stands impartial.

THRALL
And is it not accountable to community standards?

ANDY
(*voice from another room*)
You took my bubble gum away!

MRS. TOMS
(*voice from same room*)
No, I did not!

TOWERS
(*impatient*)
CUT!

END OF SHOOTING SCENE

TOWERS
(*Yelling out*)
Andy, come here!
(ANDY *enters*)
We were shooting a scene.

ANDY
Yeah, I know. I'm very sorry, Mr. Powers.

TOWERS
Mrs. Toms, get your kid some bubble gum across the street.

(HE *gestures to the door, and* ANDY *crosses to it and exits out of the library, followed by his mother*)

DAYTON
He flopped on TV. And now, our turn to sample him.

TOWERS
He did not flop on TV, Brenda, the sitcom did. The kid's edgy. Cameras love edgy. We have more important matters to be driven mad by. I got a disturbing call from some women's guild — ladies of light or something, asking question about the script.

THRALL
Oh, no.

DAYTON
Oh, yes! Bring it on!

THRALL
You are such a…
(*changing the subject*)
Sloan worried this might happen.

DAYTON
Sloan worries about Pink's Hotdogs sounding subversive. He gets anxious going into the Red Rooster.

THRALL
Very funny. Will we ever be free of McCarthy's reign?

TOWERS
Okay, we'll keep the locals in the dark, shooting a few made-up scenes to throw them off.

DAYTON
Oh, no you don't, Mr. Director. I know all about that trick. How to make hacks of us all and turn art to manure.

TOWERS
We're still shooting the script.

DAYTON

Written, really, by whom? Not really by you, Stanley?

(*an unsettling silence.* NEITHER *pushes the issue any future, as if by a secret understanding*)

By another black-listed writer hiding out under a pen name in some backwater hole over a typewriter, ghosting away for a no-name hack?

TOWERS

Brenda, Brenda, please. We are all trying to do the best we can, to get through this nightmare.

SONG: "MAKING MOVIES"

(*During the number,* THRALL, *resigned to a troubled shoot ahead, sits down and just listens to towers and* DAYTON *go at it*)

DAYTON

(*starting out slow*)

MAKING MOVIES OUGHT TO BE AS DARING AS THIS IS.

TOWERS

BRENDA, WILL YOU LISTEN?

DAYTON

YOU REWRITE IT, I'LL FIGHT IT.

TOWERS

JUST A SCENE TO SHOW YOU'RE PATRIOTIC?

DAYTON

DAYTON SINGS FOR DEWEY!

THRALL

LET'S NOT GO NUTS

DAYTON

LET'S NOT GO START MAKING CUTS!

TOWERS
FEDS ARE ASKING HAIRY QUESTIONS.

DAYTON
TELL THEM TO FLUSH OFF.

TOWERS
I CAN'T TALK THAT WAY AND KEEP COLUMBIA HAPPY.

DAYTON
COHN WANTS ME TO CRY A LOT ?

TOWERS
YOU GOT IT.

DAYTON
HELL WITH SAFE AND SAPPY.
I'LL RISK MY THROAT
FOR THE SCRIPT YOU SAY YOU WROTE.

TOWERS
WE'LL SHOOT SOME SCENES DOWN IN L.A.

DAYTON
SO COHN CAN SCREW THEM UP ?

TOWERS
HE'S BANKING IT.

DAYTON
WE SHOOT THE WHOLE THING HERE OR I QUIT.
MAKING MOVIES IS AN ART WE OUGHT TO BE PROUD OF.

TOWERS
PROUD TO BE DIRECTING YOU.

DAYTON
THEN STICK TO THE STORY.
I DID NOT AGREE TO PANDER

TOWERS
BRENDA, TRY TO...

DAYTON
DON'T PUSH ME, JOE. MAKING MOVIES…

(DAYTON *stops singing, and with script in hand, walks off to another room, with* THRALL *clapping lightly, out of respect. Now present are only* TOWERS *and* THRALL. *A phone at the check-out desk rings. towers answers it*)

TOWERS
Public library…No, this is the film company. Yes, put him through…. Sidney? Yes, we're okay…What? Rudy lives here? Are you kidding? No, I got his script through a third party, remember?…Hell, if she finds out. Are you in touch with him?…Tell him to stay away. We could all get run out of town. I will take care of Brenda…As long as we can…Okay.

(HE *hangs up the phone, turns to* THRALL)

Rudy is living right here under our noses.

THRALL
Good God, all we need is for him to make a scene.

TOWERS
He won't show his face. He's not that foolish. He's working in a furniture store under his alias. We can't let Brenda know. She would go…

(HE *is distracted by* GLORIA, *entering.* SHE *is provocatively dressed, and* HE *is instantly captured.*)

And you're the woman here for a screen test?

GLORIA
I'm Gloria Baxter, from Ladies of Light.

TOWERS
Yes, I've heard good things about your club. I love women from clubs and guilds and sewing circles. Women from canasta teams, Women on Skywatch, guarding school crosswalks, women from women from women. And you're, I'd guess, a vice president of women? Oh, Ted…

(HE *turns to* TED)

Could you go across the street, and keep an eye on Andy.

(TED *exits*)

TOWERS
And what may I do for you, Miss?

GLORIA
Baxter, Gloria. Seems your movie may not be the movie we were sold on.

TOWERS
And what were you sold?

GLORIA
Something about a juvenile delinquent turning his life around in a small town library.

TOWERS
Funny, but that sounds a lot like what I'm shooting.
(*giving her the eye*)
You look familiar. Ever do L.A.?

GLORIA
"Do" L.A.? Once.

TOWERS
Of course you did. Glamour becomes you, and I can see you in a scene we are yet to shoot inside a church. A devout believer in the American way. I'd love to audition you.

GLORIA
You would?

TOWERS
Are you game?

GLORIA
When?

TOWERS
How about later tonight, here say around eight o'clock?
(HE *eyes her ravishingly as* DAYTON *enters, giving* GLORIA *a suspicious look*)

GLORIA
How should I prepare?

TOWERS
Just be ready to make love to my cameras.

DAYTON
Haul the brat back in. I'm ready to shoot, J.T.

TOWERS
Good morning, Brenda.

(*nudging* GLORIA *off*)

Thank you for your concern. Women should be more active in civic affairs. I miss bridge now and then. I will keep you in mind.

(HE *winks at* GLORIA *behind* DAYTON'S *back. And* GLORIA *exits*)

DAYTON
I'm sure you will.

TOWERS
From Ladies of Light, asking questions. I might toss her a few lines in a bogus scene pushing apple pie virtue, to keep her quiet, and her ladies of light off our backs.

DAYTON
Or…to keep her?

(DAYTON *laughs at her own joke*)

I saw that galvanized stare out.

TOWERS
I told you, people are fishing around. We have to push virtue at every turn. You wear your happily married face, no matter. You are still married?

DAYTON
The last time I checked, and I check hourly. Yes, yes, the world must never know that my husband is — just what is he, really? And you and I

(SHE *butters up to* TOWERS)

…are not an item.

TOWERS

(*returning* DAYTON'S *flirtations*)

They must never know.

SONG: "PUBLIC RELATIONS"

(*a tango, whimsically danced by all involved*)

TOWERS

BETWEEN US, MAY I SAY YOU'RE OVERACTING A BIT?

DAYTON

BETWEEN US, YOUR DIRECTION IS SHIT.

BOTH

BUT, BABY, HOW WE FOOL 'EM IN PUBLIC RELATIONS.

DAYTON

THIS MAN HERE IS TOMORROW'S DEMILLE!

TOWERS

DIRECTING HER IS SUCH A THRILL!

DAYTON

SO FULL OF FAME AND FORTUNE,
OH, MY EGO COULD BURST

TOWERS

BUT MOTHERHOOD MUST ALWAYS COME FIRST.

DAYTON

AS FOR MY DEMON DARLINGS, WHEE!
LOVE 'EM FOR PR.

TOWERS

A STAR SHINES DOWN ON HER NURSERY.

DAYTON

JOAN CRAWFORD BABY SITS FOR ME.

(ANDY, MRS. TOMS *and* THRALL *enter*)

DAYTON AND THRALL

SELL 'EM ILLUSION.
DISH 'EM A DOSE OF GLAMOUR.
KEEP 'EM WORSHIPING OUR LIES.
FEED THEIR HUNGRY FANTASIES,
WE ARE THE WORLD THEY IDOLIZE.

THRALL

MY CASANOVA RENDEZVOUS WITH LOCALS MAKE NEWS.

TOWERS

THE SHERIFF'S NOW PATROLLING OUR CREWS.

THRALL

I ONLY CHARM THE LADIES FOR PUBLIC RELATIONS.

DAYTON

THEN GIVE YOUR FAKE FLIRTATIONS A LULL.

ANDY

(*delivering* MRS. TOMS *into* THRALL'S *reluctant arms*)

MY MOTHER IS AVAILABLE!

(THRALL *and* MRS. TOMS *tango off together*)

ACT I, SCENE 5: Brenda Dayton's hotel suite, an older room of diminishing charm.

The following Monday. **DAYTON** is sitting on the edge of the bed, holding a letter in one hand, the telephone in the other.

DAYTON

(*speaking into the phone*)

Joseph, the letter from Ladies of Light reads…

(**SHE** *reads from the letter*)

We cannot in good conscience, and as vigilant Americans, sit silently by while you lend your fame to a film that conveys sympathy for the communist way of life. And so our members urge you to leave the set.

(*nearly laughing*)

If I leave the set, it'll be by court order! (*pause*) Calm down. No, no. Have you heard of the first amendment? (*pause*) Yes, alright. Oh, don't forget, dinner at eight, the Topaz Room (*pause*) Nine is okay too.

(*She hangs up, and dials a number, and waits*)

It's Mommy, dear. Where is daddy? You don't know? Did he tell you. Did you look in his closet…Are his clothes still there? (*pause*) Some of them? Oh. well, ah…

(*The door buzzer sounds*)

Someone at the door, dear. Call you tomorrow!

(**SHE** *rises, crosses to the door. It is Jenny*)

What a lovely surprise, Jenny. Do come in!

JENNY

Oh, Miss Dayton, I am so upset, I just had to see you about the horrible letter my own mother signed her name to. I am so ashamed.

DAYTON

How sweet of you. I know you're in my court.

JENNY

And to think how nice you were, Miss Dayton, to invite ne to visit you. It is an honor to learn from an actress of your magnitude.

(*The door buzzer sounds*)

DAYTON

(*going over to answer it*)

Must be Heather Temple...Oh, how sorry I am, Jenny. I am to be interviewed. But you must come again, we will arrange.

(JENNY *crosses to the door, as* DAYTON *is opening it*)

How nice to see you again, Miss Temple. Please, do step in. My young friend, Jenny, such a promising talent, was here for some acting tips on her lines. We'll continue, Jenny.

TEMPLE

(*smiling to* JENNY)

There's a pro speaking.

JENNY

Good bye, Miss Dayton.

DAYTON

Enjoy your scenes!

(JENNY *exits*)

Please, do make yourself comfortable, Miss Temple. And what may I do for you.

TEMPLE

I have a few questions I would love to ask you, Miss Dayton.

DAYTON

So, surprise me.

TEMPLE

As you may know, your film is stirring up lively interest around town, in particular by our own Stanley Chambers.

DAYTON

Oh yes, the man who would be mayor.

TEMPLE

Would you care to comment on his claim that the movie is soft on the Communist threat?

DAYTON
Oh, my, that ever-pressing issue. Well, it's about a librarian who does her best to keep open minds open.

TEMPLE
We were informed by the Ladies of Light of a letter they wrote urging you to consider actually quitting the film. Is that correct?

DAYTON
Yes, it is. And I am glad that we live in a land where a club of intelligent women can freely compose such a fine letter. I must say, that I differ, but I do respect their feelings. And I hope that we can continue to make our movie in your lovely town.

TEMPLE
Might you share with us a little of the story itself?

DAYTON
(*as an aside*)
You know, Miss Temple, you rather remind me of a Hollywood reporter.
(TEMPLE *is flattered, and* DAYTON *continues with the question*)
The script: They make so many changes, almost daily. I can hardly keep up. I know it is not a comedy, at least not intentionally so.
(THEY *share a laugh*)
And I know it's about a librarian who inspires young minds to embrace the American way.

TEMPLE
(*taking notes*)
I see.

DAYTON
And quite a challenge for me to be playing a part off my usual…course.
(SHE *laughs a little,* TEMPLE *grants her a few polite giggles*)

TEMPLE
No Jezebel on the set?

DAYTON
No, Jezebel is now turning her life around in the closed stacks — that is, as long as they're closed.

(THEY *share a larger laugh, then* DAYTON *picks up sheet music from a side table*)

But Jezebel may soon be back — on Broadway in a musical revue, *The Wrong People Love Me.*

TEMPLE
Oh, my!

DAYTON
The title song. Producer just sent me to learn. He thinks I'm the perfect one to introduce it.

TEMPLE
You sing too?

DAYTON
Oh, I've done Broadway, hon.

TEMPLE
Well, you do keep busy. On a lighter note, how do you cope with being away from family for such long periods?

DAYTON
It's not easy, I miss them so. You might say I am living two lives. Your questions inspire me to think deeper, Hedda — *I mean Heather…*

(*waves her hand, as if a signal she is waiting for another question*)

SONG: "PUBLIC RELATIONS"

TEMPLE

(*as if, perhaps, having been sucked into the theatricality of* DAYTON'S *world*)

HOW DOES THE MODERN WOMAN BALANCE HOME AND CAREER?

DAYTON
SHE JUGGLES ROLES LIKE TRUZZI, MY DEAR.
BUT ONE THING DOESN'T CHANGE,
I'M HOME EVERY THANKSGIVING,
TO PLUCK AND STUFF AND BASTE THE OLD HEN.
I'M VERY MUCH THE HOUSEWIFE THEN.

TEMPLE
HOW DOES YOUR HUSBAND DEAL WITH YOUR ROUSING SUCCESS?

DAYTON
HE LOVES MY ROUSING PAYCHECKS, I GUESS.
AND STILL I LET HIM THINK WITHOUT HIS LOVE
(*melodramatically*)
I'M NOTHING.

TEMPLE
(*suddenly wrapping up her notes, rising and crossing to the door*)
YOU'VE GIVEN ME RARE INSIGHT IN YOU,
(TEMPLE *opens the door*)
THAT WAS A LOVELY INTERVIEW!
Thank you, Miss Dayton!

(TEMPLE *exits, leaving* DAYTON *aghast over her abrupt departure*)

DAYTON
(*standing there, feeling semi stood-up*)
What? That's all? Temple, you are no Hedda!
(SHE *surveys her now empty suite, picks up the ringing telephone*)
Stan, yes, really? You can't make it?
(*long pause*)
What about nine o'clock then?…Ten o'clock? Anytime?
(*listens, then turns angry*)
And what do you expect me to do, holed up here all by myself while everybody else is out whooping it up?
(*pause*)
Yes, of course. No, I don't understand! Stay up all night with the bimbo, for all I care!

(SHE *hangs up the telephone and sits there in a gloomy funk, looks at the sheet music, studies it as music in background teases her into giving it a try. She picks up the phone and sings into it*)

SONG: "THE WRONG PEOPLE LOVE ME"

**DIAL UP A BLUE SONG:
WHO'S DOING WHO SONG?
THE WHOLE DAMN CREW SONG,
BUT NO ONE IS COOING MY WAY.
IS THERE LOVE THAT'S EVERLASTING
IN CENTRAL CASTING?**

(SHE *picks up a necklace off an end table, dangles it indifferently from her fingers, and lets it drop onto the floor,* SHE *is now using the phone as if it were a mic, holding it in one hand, the lead sheet in the other*)

**JEWELRY FROM CRAWFORD.
FLOWERS FROM CRAWFORD.
DEATH THREATS FROM CRAWFORD.
THE WRONG PEOPLE LOVE ME, DEAR LORD.
I'M SO DESPERATE I'D GO STEADY
WITH NELSON EDDY.**

(SHE *lets go of the phone, and wings the rest*)

**I'M SO IN NEED OF
A MAN WHOSE SENSITIVE AND DEEP.
STILL, I PREFER THE COMMON CAD
OVER THE LADDIE WHO SINGS BROADWAY IN HIS SLEEP.**

**TODD SEEMED IDEAL,
THE PERFECT HEAL,
HE DID NOT STEAL.
AT LAST, LOVE WITH HONOR, BUT THEN
TODD STAYED TRUE TO WHAT HE WAS, AND
HE STOLE MY HUSBAND.**

SAMMY WAS SMITTEN,
I WAS HIS KITTEN.
WHEN I TRIED FLITTEN,
"TILL DEATH DO US PART," SAMMY CRIED.
SO TO "PART," ONE NIGHT I THRILLED HIM,
UNTIL IT KILLED HIM.

OLD STAR UNWANTED,
OLD STAR WHOSE HAUNTED EVERY DIVE.
FRIENDS SAY, "BE GLAD YOU'RE STILL ALIVE"
I SAY, EXCUSE ME,
BUT ALONE IS NOT ALIVE!

I AM THE DOLE NOW
FOR EVERY SOUL NOW
WHO'S ON PAROLE NOW.
THE WRONG PEOPLE LOVE ME, WHO NEXT?
LET THEM LOVE ME ANY WAY NOW
HEY, JOAN, OLE NOW!

ACT I, SCENE 6: Interior scene at the library check-out counter.

Wednesday, two days later. Present are GLORIA, reading from a script in hand, and THRALL, the two acting in a scene being filmed. MRS. TOMS, seated, observes with a little envy.

SHOOTING SCENE

GLORIA (*playing a churchgoer on the amateurish side*)
I respect good books, too, Pastor Thorn, but I believe our city fathers have a duty to expose and root out subversive literature that can infect young minds.

THRALL (*as the pastor*)
Bless you, my child. You are what this town needs more of.

GLORIA
My faith is the rock on which…

(ANDY *bursts in*)

ANDY
Who stole my Popeye Power Pops?

TOWERS
You're interrupting a screen test, Andy!

CUT!

END OF SHOOTING SCENE

TOWERS
(*To* ANDY)
Okay, after we shoot the next scene, your mother can take you over to Thrifty's and buy the whole damn candy counter, on me! Now go back there and wait.

(ANDY *exits, to the side room, followed by* MRS. TOMS)

THRALL

(*following the two,* HE *exits*)

Any donuts left?

TOWERS

(*to* GLORIA)

You did very well, Miss Baxter. You're a quick take.

ANDY'S VOICE

(*yelling, from the other room*)

My nuts are not your nuts!

TOWERS

(*To* GLORIA)

Why don't you have a seat over there and watch us shoot the next scene.

(SHE *complies, and* HE *exits to the side room*)

Child actors! Be back shortly.

(GLORIA, *taking advantage of being alone, looks around with probing curiosity, goes to the check out desk and picks up a book, and is startled by the title, not visible to the audience, starts to ruffle through the pages like a defective, hears voices, puts the book back down, and hurries back to a chair. Moments later,* DAYTON *enters, with script in hand, noticing* GLORIA *with suspicion, but without comment.*)

DAYTON

Joseph!

TOWERS

(*returning with* THRALL)

Perfect timing, Brenda. We're ready to shoot.

(DAYTON goes around the desk, sits down and places the script upon it)

Okay, scene thirty nine! (*Calling out*) Andy, are you ready?

ANDY
(*calling out from another room*)
Yes!

TOWERS
Gum out of your mouth?

ANDY
Yes!

TOWERS
Lights, camera, action!

SHOOTING SCENE

(ANDY *enters, with book in hand, and goes to check it out*)

DAYTON
Well, what will it be today, Rusty?

ANDY (*as Rusty*)
I'm in a very patriotic mood, Miss Lake, touched by warm feelings all over town for the love-America display at city hall.

(HE *hands her a book for check out*)

DAYTON
Fathers of Freedom. You've chosen well, and I'm proud.
(SHE *stamps the book and hands it to* ANDY)

ANDY
Thanks to your stimulating influence, Miss Lake! My mom calls you a pillar of the community.

DAYTON
(*faking the mild onset of a tear or two*)
And I am touched, Rusty. Helping to guide young minds onto the path of our divinely inspired way of life fills my heart with all that's good and true, and...

ANDY

(*acting overly emotional*)

And you make going to the library better than the most fantastic mew carnival ride at the county fair.

DAYTON

(*Getting more emotional, wiping a fake tear from her eye*)

...your eager words, how they move me in these troubled times, when all around are shadows of an unsettling force out there.

(SHE *starts to cry, and then struggles to hold back a giggle*)

TOWERS

(*intervening*)

CUT!

END OF SHOOTING SCENE

DAYTON

(*a snickering aside to* TOWERS)

Loretta Young.

ANDY

I get to go to Thrifty's!

(ANDY *and* MRS. TOMS *exit*)

TOWERS

(*to* GLORIA)

Alright, Gloria. You should be hearing from us soon.

GLORIA

(*rising to leave*)

Thank you, Joseph.

(SHE *exits*)

DAYTON

Joseph?

TOWERS
Yes, Joseph. She's on our side, now. She'll talk up the two bogus scenes I just shot, the first one, her so-called screen test, and then let's see what they say about our patriotism.

DAYTON
(*laughing a little*)
I'll give you credit, Joseph. You wrote that? I think they're looking for a cutting edge writer over at *Father Knows Best.*

TOWERS
Brenda, brace yourself for what I am about to say.

DAYTON
You're turning us into a musical?

TOWERS
No, Rudy Engler wrote the script.

DAYTON
Rudy Engler?

TOWERS
Yes, Rudy.

DAYTON
Oh, God, bless Rudy and his typewriter wherever they are.

TOWERS
They are here in Rosa Valley.

DAYTON
Rudy is here, working on the script?

TOWERS
No, he lives here, under a different name.

DAYTON
I can't believe this. I've got to see him.

TOWERS
No, you don't, and you won't. You try finding him, and all of us are ruined. That hysterical politician will crucify us. Rudy is a blacklisted writer, Brenda. Had I known he moved here, I'd have scouted another location.

(JENNY *enters, excitedly, stops to see if she is interrupting a scene.* TOWERS *smiles*)

JENNY
Good news, Miss Dayton! They're inviting you to be in the Rosa Valley Days parade next Saturday!

THRALL
Oh, I love a parade!

DAYTON
Well, that's nice of them.

TOWERS
And who invited us?

(MRS. TOMS *and* ANDY *return*)

JENNY
The vice mayor, Sam Sparling. He asked me to deliver the invitation.
(*to* MRS. TOMS *and* ANDY)
They want us to be in the parade!

MRS. TOMS
Oh, won't that be grand!

ANDY
(*making a face*)
Yeah, mom, real grand.

THRALL
Bands and majorettes, horses, crisp, stout drill teams. Big fat floats smothered in flowers.

TOWERS
Okay, Ted!

JENNY
Oh, Andy, they asked me to see if you would sing a song about duck and cover at the festival show after the parade. I have a copy of it with me.

THRALL
(*to self*)
Prime publicity.

ANDY
I don't do musicals.

MRS. TOMS
You do now. He will, Jenny! He's just a little shy in the singing department.

ANDY
(*to* MRS. TOMS)
I'm no tap-dancing banana!

MRS. TOMS
Shhh! You're thinking Pasadena.

(*The focus falls now onto* JENNY *and* DAYTON, *the latter seeming to be lost in some kind of mystical musing.* JENNY *draws closer to* DAYTON, *intrigued*)

JENNY
Your presence here is making our town a better town, Miss Dayton.

DAYTON
It's all in the writing, Jenny.

JENNY
The writing?

DAYTON
The words on paper. Sometimes they say nothing to me. Other times, they inspire me in many ways, and I live for them.

ANDY
I don't sing, mother!

MRS. TOMS
You will, or else!

JENNY
(*having approached* DAYTON)
We've never had a person as famous as you, Miss Dayton, march in our parade. What an honor it would be.

DAYTON
Then let me honor you, Jenny. Would you sit by my side in an open car?

JENNY
Of course, I would. I would go anywhere with you, Miss Dayton. Remember how you felt that first day you came to Rosa Valley? When You said you wanted to be just like the rest of us and walk down real streets.

DAYTON
How I would love to be...part of something bigger than...
(SHE *looks around the set as a symbol of her life*)

SONG: "MY PARADE"

MY PARADE BEGINS WITH ROSES ON A FLOAT
SHADES OF RED, WHITE AND BLUE.
AND THEY BLOSSOM IN ALL COLORS AND ALL CREEDS,
EVERY STRIPE, EVERY HUE.
DON'T BE DISILLUSIONED SITTING ON THE SIDELINES,
STAND UP, AT LAST, AND MAKE YOUR FEELINGS KNOWN.
BEAT A DRUM FOR YOUR CONVICTIONS,
YOU MAY FIND YOU'RE NOT ALONE.

MY PARADE IS UNAFRAID TO SING A SONG,
DARK AS DEATH, RED AS RAGE,
FOR MY COLLEAGUES WHO WERE CENSORED, ONE BY ONE,
OUT OF WORDS, OFF THE STAGE.
I SALUTE THEM ALL WHO STOOD UP TO INJUSTICE

AND ANSWERED, "NO, WE WILL NOT SHARE YOUR SHAME!"
I PARADE FOR FRIENDS IMPRISONED
WHO REFUSED TO NAME MY NAME.
WHEN FREE SOULS AREN'T FREE TO SPEAK THEIR MINDS,
IS THIS AMERICA?
DO WE LIGHT THE WORLD BY BURNING BOOKS
OR HAVE WE LOST OUR WAY?
MY PARADE REFUSES TO RETREAT
FROM A FAR STAR SPANGLED DREAM I QUOTE:
WHO ARE THEY WHO MAKE DEMOCRACY LIVE OR DIE?
YOU AND I.
MY PARADE BEGINS WITH ROSES ON A FLOAT,
SHADES OF RED, WHITE AND BLUE.

(SHE *walks off.* OTHERS *look on in quiet respect*)

ACT II, SCENE 1: A small outdoor stage in a park setting. A banner overhead reads Rosa Valley Days.

The following Saturday. Scene is preceded by a crossover march on the stage apron. Parading locals are adorned in roses.

SONG: "THE COMMUNITY MARCH"

A FEW LOCALS

RAISE A ROSE TO THE SUN,
PUT THE PRUNE ON PROUD DISPLAY,
BEAT THE DRUM FOR THE PLUM.
WHO IS NUMBER ONE?
ROSA VALLEY, ALWAYS IN BLOOM
RAINBOW CORN —
THORNLESS ROSE —
PRAISE THE MAN WHO MADE THEM GROW:
HERBERT LUTHER WHO SANG
WHEN HE CAME OUT WEST,
ROSA VALLEY SOIL IS BEST!

(THEY *march off as lights rise on the small stage, upstage center. The songs performed upon it can spill out downstage*)

ANNOUNCER'S VOICE

Rosa Valleyans, have we got a treat for you! From the popular TV hit, Teenage Times, one of the co-stars of the movie now being filmed at our own library, and his mother, who considers herself an amateur — but we love amateurs, don't we! Let's give a big hand to Andy and Mrs Toms singing for civil defense!

SONG: "DUCK AND COVER"

(MRS. TOMS *throws herself into the number.* ANDY *turns it almost into a spoof of itself by his awkwardly — or purposely — overdone movements.* HE *does seem to be having a good time, whatever his intent. The first lines are more rhythmically spoken*)

ANDY
ONE DAY AT SCHOOL YOUR HEAR JETS ROAR.

MRS. TOMS
THE CEILING SHAKES BUT YOU STAY CALM.

ANDY
YOUR CLASSMATES ALL SHOULD BE...

MRS. TOMS
INSIDE.
AND IF THEY AREN'T YOU YELL H BOMB!

BOTH
(going into the song)
GET DOWN,
DO THE DUCK AND COVER!
GET DOWN,
HIT THE FLOOR AND HOVER!
FOLLOW THIS RULE,
YOU'LL BE RADIOACTIVE FREE.

MRS. TOMS
BOMBS BURST

ANDY
DO THE DUCK AND COVER!
HEAD FIRST,
UNDERNEATH A TABLE

BOTH
WINNING THE WAR FOR IKE,
COMMIES GO TAKE A HIKE!

(MRS. TOMS, *nearly out of breath, struggles to keep up with* ANDY'S *attack. This could be a production number, with some of the* SPECTATORS *joining in)*

ANDY
BOMBS BURST
DO THE DUCK AND COVER

MRS. TOMS
HEAD FIRST
HIT THE FLOOR AND HOVER

ANDY
(*going risqué*)
DOWN WHERE THE FALLEN FLIRT
DURING A RED ALERT!
(MRS. TOMS *pinches his arm, as if they are in a vaudeville act and* SHE *is taking him to task for vulgarity*)

MRS. TOMS
STAY THERE AND DON'T YOU FLIRT

BOTH
DOING THE RED ALERT!
(*Some applause and cheers, as* ANDY *milks the crowd, at the same time making weird faces*)

ANNOUNCER (voice only)
Aren't they wonderful, folks! Hollywood pros! And here comes our very own little theatre star, who is now filming scenes in the movie…Jenny Crane!
(JENNY *enters, her face aglow, to scattered applause*)
Jenny would like to honor pioneering women, whose spirit, she believes, Brenda Dayton is fearlessly keeping alive!

SONG: "MISS TOMORROW"

JENNY
WHO CAN BURP A BABY WHILE SHE STUDIES PLATO
MISS TOMORROW CAN.
DNA UNCOVERED BY ONE SHARP TOMATO
NONE WERE SMARTER THAN
NOW SHE DRIVES A CAR, TOO,
TAKES THE NEW YORK BAR, TOO,
AND STILL WARMS DADDY'S ROLL.
DON'T YOU RAIN ON YOUR JANE,
OR SHE MAY STROLL.

SHE HAS HIDDEN ASSETS,
UNDISCOVERED TALENTS,
BETTER TREAT HER RIGHT.
SHE WAS ROSIE RIVETER, A WARTIME WELDER
WHO TOMORROW MIGHT
WELD HER NEW-FOUND YEARNINGS
TO THE WORLD OF EARNINGS
AND END UP C.E.O.
THERE'S NO STOPPING HER NOW, SHE'S ON THE GO!
SHE WAS EARHART FLYING,
MARY PLEASANT FIGHTING FOR THE SLAVES TO BE FREE,
MOLLY PITCHER GUNNING,
MRS. WOODHULL RUNNING FOR THE PRESIDENCY!

NELLY BLY EXPOSED HOW PRISONS TORTURED HER,
AND SUFFRAGETTES CLOSED RANK.
BOYS AND GIRLS REMOVED FROM SWEAT SHOP
MINES AND MILLS
HAVE MOTHER JONES TO THANK.
WHO INVENTED PHYSICS.
BRAS AND SEEING EYE DOGS,
AND ICE CREAM CONE DESIGN?
MISS TOMORROW IS WHO!
TAKE A BOW, LADY KNOW HOW.
TRUST WHATEVER YOU'RE DOING,
YOU'RE DOING JUST FINE!

(*fair applause, including a cat call or two*)

It is my great pleasure and honor to introduce Brenda Dayton!

(DAYTON *enters amidst scattered cheers and a few grumbles*)

DAYTON

Thank you everyone, you have all been so lovely to me, and this is a film I will long remember working on, given your beautiful town and warm reception. And I must thank Jenny Crane for riding in the parade with me, and for all your smiles along the way! It almost felt like I had made it back to Grauman's Chinese theatre for another world premiere!

DISGRUNTLED VOICE IN THE CROWD

Miss Dayton! Miss Dayton!

(SHE *looks out to see who it might be*)

Is your movie about how to be a communist?

DAYTON

(*taken aback*)

Well, far from. It is a movie about the challenges a librarian faces in the modern age.

ANOTHER VOICE IN THE CROWD

Chambers for mayor!

DAYTON

And I can you see you have a very active political campaign going on, a very good sign for the health of our democracy in your community.

DISGRUNTLED VOICE

Miss Dayton! Are you a...

ANOTHER VOICE

Let her speak!

(DAYTON *holds back, politely, waiting for* DISGRUNTLED VOICE *to speak.* THRALL *comes up and whispers something in her ear*)

DAYTON

I hope to get to know you more before our filming ends. As you know, some of your are appearing in the movie as extras, and who knows, some of those extras may one day be names on a marquee!

(*turning to* JENNY)

Here is a young woman whom, I believe, could go all the way.

DISGRUNTLED VOICE
(*just shouting*)
You ever were a communist?

OTHER VOICE
She's an actress, fool!

OTHER VOICE
She's not a politician.

DISGRUNTLED VOICE
Another one of those unmarried librarians!

DAYTON
(*Growing uncomfortable, as* THRALL *leans her way and whispers something else into her ear*)
Oh, Ted Thrall tells me I am expected back at the library for more shooting. And, so, I shall thank you all…
(*some polite cheers, a hiss or too*)
And wish you a great festival day!

(THRALL *guides the slightly shaken* DAYTON *down the steps off the small platform, to downstage right, to make an exit. Sounds of cheers and heckling can be heard, and the hecklers increase slightly to an ominous pitch.*

JENNY, *who has been standing on the platform watching it all, at the last moment, just after* DAYTON *and* THRALL *have exited, goes down the steps and follows after them. Lights alter to focus on her.*

BILL *enters from upstage, holding a pro-Chambers poster or placard, and crosses to* JENNY, *letting the sign drop so she can't easily see it*)

BILL
Jenny! Where have you been? I've been trying to reach you, You're never in when I call.
(SHE *spots a* CHAMBERS *pin on his shirt*)
I'm sorry if this bothers you. Stanley Chambers will be here long after the film company leaves town. And he has promised me a position in his administration if he wins.

JENNY
Is that it? How could you march with his supporters in a parade like this?

BILL
I told Mr. Chambers I could not march with his group if they were going to protest the movie, and he agreed. And they didn't.

JENNY
But did you hear those cruel questions shouted out at her?

(BILL *remains mum*)

Those are the people voting for Chambers!

BILL
How do you know, Jenny? This whole thing is turning into…Look, it's not a perfect world, and I can't say I like everything about him, but the mayor we have has never impressed me. And there are enemies within. It's a dangerous time. Can't you see?

JENNY
Yes. I see. Because of this nasty election, you walk off the set? I would never do anything like that.

BILL
I did not walk off the set, I was only an extra, I had no more lines.

BILL
How would you know unless you stuck around? To get even one line in a movie shows real talent.

BILL
Jenny. Please, try to see it my way. This should not come between us, I hope. There's a group marching for our Mayor. Why don't you join them?

(JENNY, *frozen in ambivalence, softens some to* BILL'S *suggestion, and he tries to kiss her, but hesitates*)

I would be proud to see you supporting the mayor.

(SHE *starts to see him differently*)

Can I see you after the parade, for lunch? For a walk. I'll look for you right here, Jenny, in case. You are the only one.

(JENNY *tries to show* BILL *some respect, half a smile, and walks off*)

SONG: "IN HER MAGIC"

BILL
HOW SAD MY SONG SINGS WITHOUT HER,
HOW LONELY THE NOTES NOW FEEL.
HOW SAD TO FIGHT FOR A FEELING
THAT YESTERDAY SEEMED SO REAL.

THE DAYS WE DANCED IN THE SUNSHINE,
THE WINTERS WE LAUGHED AWAY.
WERE THEY A DREAM BUT IN PASSING?
SWEET FANTASY, WON'T YOU STAY...
ONE MORE CHANCE, PLEASE.
MORE ROMANCE, PLEASE!

WHAT WENT WRONG?
WAS I LOST IN THE SONG,
TOO FOOLED BY A BRIGHT REFRAIN?
NOW ALONE, I WILL PRAY AND BELIEVE
MY HEARTACHE WAS NOT IN VAIN.

I WRAPPED MYSELF IN HER MAGIC.
NOW LONGINGLY, I REPLAY
THE LOVE I FOUND WHEN SHE ENTERED —
SAME SETTING, SAME LIGHT, SAME SMILE.
ONE MORE TAKE, PLEASE.
HEART, DON'T BREAK PLEASE!

(HE *looks down upon his pro-Chambers sign, picks it up pitifully, and slowly walks off*)

ACT II, SCENE 2: The library interior.

The following Tuesday. Present is **TOWERS**, sitting at a table and reading a newspaper. We hear the voices of **MRS. TOMS** and **ANDY**, as they enter.

MRS. TOMS
Don't forget, Andy, I was somebody before I ever went out to Hollywood.

ANDY
Where, mother, in Bakersfield?

MRS. TOMS
(*hopping to impress* TOWERS)
We're getting calls from agents. And I don't care what you say, Andy, you're a born hoofer. You missed your true calling in vaudeville.

ANDY
Vaudeville! What are you smoking?

MRS. TOMS
Button your lips!

TOWERS
(*Looking*)
Another Mickey Rooney. I read it in the paper, Andy. You should be thrilled over the reception.
(*holds up paper, reading*)
Brenda Dayton and Andy Toms, big hits at Rosa Valley Days.

MRS. TOMS
I told Andy he could do it.

(THRALL *enters*)

THRALL
More not good news, Joseph. Ernie says you can't shoot outside the mayor's house. City Hall is going dark on us.

TOWERS
Damn those finks!

THRALL
If you were running for mayor against Chambers, would you want us in your front yard? Ernie's found something on McDonald Avenue.

TOWERS
Where Hitchcock filmed Shadow?

THRALL
(*laughing*)
Oh, the irony of it all! The story we're shooting is damn near the story we're living! Just who is imitating whom?

(DAYTON *enters*)

DAYTON
Me, of course. Joseph, we won the parade! Did you see the front page in today's paper? Picture perfect. My most misleading profile in years.

TOWERS
Don't be too sure, dearest Brenda. They might run us back to a sound stage.

MRS. TOMS
Oh, Miss Dayton, did you hear that the talent show was cancelled?

(*Surprise to* DAYTON *the* OTHERS)

DAYTON
No, I didn't.

MRS. TOMS
Something about too many people who usually enter all being on vacation.

THRALL
We might have the whole town to ourselves.

DAYTON

(*surprisingly, a little humbled*)

Oh, and I was…

(SHE *stops, unable to reveal her disappointment, sits down at a table, and tries to lose herself in the newspaper*)

TOWERS

(*sensing her deflation*)

Brenda, you handled yourself with great dignity at the parade, there were bound to be hecklers.

THRALL

I'm sure you'll shine, Brenda, at your beauty tips presentation.

DAYTON

(*not much lifted*)

That still on? Now I work the drug store circuit, if they don't axe it, too. (*pause*) Tiffany's to Thrifty's. (*pause*) I draw the line at Woolworth's.

(SHE *rises*)

And I don't do Maytag tie-ins.

(SHE *rises and exits into another room*)

ANDY

(*muttering*)

Loser.

TOWERS

Loser. And just what are you? Another child actor, in a few dreary years with any luck, an aging child star fighting off suicide in minor roles, envious extras gloating over your downfall, as if to be snickering, "Go ahead, hang yourself from a palm tree!"

ANDY

Maybe I will.

MRS. TOMS

Andy!

TOWERS

Or you could make "Duck and Cover" your signature song and have a whole career, running up to ads for Popeye Power Pops.

ANDY

I'll hang from a tree first.

SONG: "MAKE 'EM SCREAM"

WHEN I'M A STAR
I'LL MURDER THEM
IF I END UP AT MGM
IN MOVIE MUSICALS.
I'M ROBBING BANKS,
I'M RUNNING GANGS,
I'M KICKING ASS,
I'M GROWING FANGS —
I'M STICKING TO DRAMA!

MAKE 'EM SCREAM!
MAKE 'EM SWOON!
GIVE 'EM GORE,
BE A GOON!

I'M NOT ASTAIRE.
MY LEGS EXTEND,
I SPIRAL OFF
(HE *puts the song to the most bizarre anti graceful choreography*)
WHAT DOESN'T BEND
BEGINS TO TURN ON ME.
DID SOMETHING CRACK?
THIS ISN'T FUN.
MY POSTURING, UNDONE. BEGETS
A PRETZEL IN MOTION.
"ARCH YOUR BACK!"
ARCH MY WHAT?
"HIPS IN LINE!"
WHERE'S MY BUTT?

DIG MY RHYTHM, IS IT PLAIN
I'M NOT DANCING IN THE RAIN?
IN MY DIAPERS, LEARNED TO TAP.
TO THE BEAT I TOOK A CRAP

WHEN I'M A STAR,
IT'S PAY BACK TIME
FOR ALL THE SAPS
WHO SAY THAT I'M
THE FRANKENSTEIN OF TAPS.
MY MOTHER, WHO
HATES HOLLYWOOD,
FOR LAYING HER,
IS PAYING ME
TO TORTURE DIRECTORS.
WHAT A BLAST DISHING SAS —
MAYER, YOU'RE FULL OF GAS!

NO DING DING DONG
LIKE JUDY WENT.
I'D RATHER RIDE AN ELEPHANT
THAN FLY WHERE BLUE BIRDS FLY.
OR KNOCK 'EM DEAD LIKE MAMMA TRIED.
I'LL MAKE 'EM LAUGH,
IN HOMICIDE, I'M FIT AS A FIDDLE.

BUSBY BERKELEY, I REFUSE
TO BEHAVE IN DANCING SHOES.
I WON'T DANCE,
I WON'T CROON,
QUAKE AND SHAKE
MAKE 'EM SCREAM!

ACT II, SCENE 3: The front steps of the library.

Thursday, two days later. THRALL enters through the door to discover a small gaggle of protestors in the distance with placards, shouting.

SHOOTING SCENE

THRALL
Oh, no! This can't be!

(THRALLS *watches as protesters, of whom there are but a few, march up to stand in front of the steps. One placard reads* "BETTER DEAD THAN RED!", *another* "ASSAULT ON DEMOCRACY ASSAULT" *and another* "FIRE PINKO BOOK PUSHER!")

SONG: "PROTEST SONG"

PROTESTERS
GIVE HER THE BOOT!
SHOW HER THE DOOR!
COMMIE GO HOME!
COMMIE NO MORE!
OFF OF OUR STREETS,
OUT OF OUR SCHOOLS,
GET 'EM BEFORE TYRANNY RULES!

WHAT IS SHE HIDING? WHERE DID SHE COME FROM?
WHO DOES SHE TALK TO DOWN IN THE CITY?
RALLY FOR YOUTH,
FIGHT FOR THE TRUTH NOW!
SHOW HER WHOSE BOSS.
SHE WHO DEFIES
ORDERS TO BAN COMUNIST LIES!
HOW IS SHE PAID?
OUT OF OUR TAX!
WHAT DO WE GET?
COMMUNIST TRACTS!

WE MUST PRESERVE COMMUNITY STANDARDS.
HARRIET LAKE IS HARBORING BAND WORDS.
FIGHT FOR THE FACTS.
GIVE HER THE AXE NOW!
HER REIGN MUST END
IT'S A DISGRACE
WE MUST REPLACE LAKE

OLD WOMAN
She's no friend of ours!

PROTESTORS
HOW DARE THEY TRASH OUR LOVELY TOWN,
THEY SHOULD BE SHUT DOWN !
OUT WITH HER BOOKS!
OFF WITH HER HEAD!
GETTING TOO SMART!
ACTING TO RED!
WHERE IS SHE FROM?
WHO DOES SHE KNOW?
IS SHE A FRIEND?
IS SHE A FOE?
TIME TO REMOVE THE BLIGHT FROM OUR BOOK SHELVES,
TIME TO RECLAIM AMERICAN VALUES!

(BRENDA DAYTON *comes out through the front door.* THRALL *escorts her protectively*)

THRALL
(*waving his arms*)
Please! Quiet for a moment, everyone! Let our librarian respond!
(*The* CROWD *calms down*)

SONG: "PLEASE DON'T CRY FOR ME"

DAYTON
PLEASE DON'T CRY FOR ME, ROSA VALLEY,
MY LIBRARIANSHIP MAY END.

**NO, DON'T HECKLE MY FALSE ACCUSERS UNTIL THEY
GIVE ME MY SEVERANCE PAY.**

**THOUGH AGAINST MY BELIEFS YOU RALLY,
STILL, I CHERISH YOUR EARLY PRAISE —
HOW, YOU STATED, TO QUOTE "SHE SHINES CROSS INDEXING,
SHE MADE THE DATE STAMP SING"**

**DID I ERR PUSHING CHAUCER?
DID I ERR SHOWING SINGLE MEN
"FRIENDLY PLEASURES FROM BANGKOK"
SIX SIX NINE POINT F - U - N.**

**IF YOU'LL PARDON ME, ROSA VALLEY,
I MUST ANSWER NOW TO THE WORLD.
YES. I'LL GET BY,
SO LET MY MARTYRDOM BEGIN.
IS LITERATURE A SIN?**

SOME PROTESTERS	SOME SUPPORTERS
Yes! Yes! Yes!	No! No! No!
IS SHE A FRIEND?	**HARRIET LAKE!**
IS SHE A FOE?	**HARRIET LAKE!**

(GLORIA *rushes up, with mike in hand*)

GLORIA

(*playing a reporter*)

Miss Lake, there are rumors that you've been let go?

(DAYTON *remains stoically non committal*)

THRALL (*as Hank*)

Miss Lake is still the librarian. This is an issue yet to be taken up by city hall when the mayor returns from Washington.

A YOUNG VOICE IN THE CROWD

Please don't go, Miss Lake!

DAYTON

(*obviously touched*)

But if I do, you will understand in time, my dear.

I MAY CRY FOR YOU ROSA VALLEY
WHEN REPORTERS DISCOVER HOW
I WAS INTERVIEWED BY THE CHAIRMAN OF THE BOARD,
DOWN WHERE OLD BOOKS ARE STORED.
DON'T BE TEARYEYED SHOULD YOU FIND ME
WASHING WINDOWS OR WALKING STREETS,
IF THE CAR HOP YOU GET AT ETHEL'S EAT & RUN
WAS YOUR LIBRARIAN.

DON'T DESPISE MY REPLACEMENT
SHOULD SHE OFFER YOU FREE BALLOONS.
SHE WILL COMFORT YOUR CHILDREN
WITH HER LOVE OF LOONY TUNES.
PLEASE DON'T CRY FOR ME ROSA VALLEY.
CRY, INSTEAD, FOR THE LIGHTS THAT BURN.
CRY FOR CATHER AND BLAKE,
FOR SHAKESPEARE AND SPILLANE.
AND IF YOUR MINDS WERE MOVED
MY WORK WAS NOT IN VAIN!

(*The startling* apparent *imposition of reality here, as a can or rock or hard object can be heard smashing against glass. Actors are rattled, but towers motions everyone to keep the scene going*)

DAYTON

The shock of a rock, may I address that?

GLORIA

(*whispering into her mike*)

She's about to make what almost sounds unscripted.

DAYTON

Yes, I am everybody (*dramatic pause*) How best to serve the people of this community? Though we are but one small town on the American map, yet within these hallowed walls, these walls that Carnegie gave us, we travel the same world together. We rise to the highest level of mankind's quest for knoweldge. And we send our sons and daughters out into the world, prepared to fight for the freedoms we hold dear to our hearts — the freedoms that a library should faithfully preserve. And since I have become an obstacle in its path, I am, effective now, stepping aside.

GLORIA

(*into her mike*)

She's leaving, she says.

SOME

No, no, Miss Lake!

UNSEEN VOICE

Good riddance!

(ANDY *wraps his arms around her legs*)

You can't leave us, Miss Lake! I won't let you go!

DAYTON

Allow me one last referral, Andy...All books

NO, DON'T CRY FOR ME, ROSA VALLEY
CRY, INSTEAD, FOR THE LIGHTS THAT BURN
CRY FOR TWAIN AND THOREAU
FOR CHRISTIE AND CAMUS
FOR THOSE WHO READ TO LEARN
I LEAVE MY BOOKS TO YOU!

(SHE *looks back one last time at the library, and then exits through the crowd.* JENNY *and* ANDY *follow her*)

TOWERS

CUT!

END OF SHOOTING SCENE

ACT II, SCENE 4: Dayton's empty hotel suite.

The following Saturday evening.

RADIO ANNOUNCERS VOICE
In local news, two male teenagers were arrested near the library earlier today for causing a disturbance during film shooting. Police Chief Marvin "Mitch" Moore offering maximum security for the film company. Mayoral candidate Stanley Chambers claiming incriminating evidence in the form of a book titled *The Case for Communism,* found on the set by an undisclosed source.

(DAYTON *enters the room in a night dress, turns off the radio. A mass of paint and manure crash against the window, nearly breaking it*)

UNSEEN PROTESTERS' VOICES
(*from offstage*)
WHERE IS SHE FROM!
WHO DOES SHE KNOW!
IS SHE A FRIEND!
IS SHE A FOE!

(*Startled,* DAYTON, *moves away from the window, and is driven to lie down on the bed and burry her head in the pillows*)

OFF OF OUR STREETS!
OUT OF OUR SCHOOLS!
(HUAC *voices are heard only*)

HUAC VOICE
Miss Dayton, did you not attend a Communist party meeting on December 14, 1938?

ANOTHER HUAC VOICE
Miss Dayton, will you please answer the question!

HUAC VOICE
Are you or were you ever a member of the Communist party?

DAYTON
No, no, no!

ANOTHER HUAC VOICE
Do you know Rudy Engler, Miss Dayton?

HUAC VOICE
You may be charged with contempt of Congress!

ANOTHER HUAC VOICE
Do you or do you not know a Rudy Engler?

HUAC VOICE
What can you tell us about Rudy Engler?

DAYTON
You blacklisted Rudy Engler!

HUAC VOICE
To repeat, are you now or were you ever a member of the Communist party?

DAYTON
(*shouting out*)
Have you nothing better to do?

(SHE *crosses to the window and opens it*)

No, I will not answer the question! No I will not be a part
of your witch hunt. No, no, a thousand times no!

(SHE *hears a siren in the distance, shuts the window, and sits on the bed*)

SONG: "FALLEN STAR"

(*We hear* JENNY *singing the song, in voice only, or beyond a scrim in which case, her image is ghostly.* DAYTON *hears her, too, and she crosses to a dresser and picks up a small photo, and takes comfort in the image*)

JENNY'S VOICE
FALLEN STAR,
YOU LIVED THE LIFE THEY IDOLIZE.
NOW SOMEONE KNOCKS YOU DOWN TO SIZE.
FATE COMES AND GOES LIKE THAT.

FANS ACCLAIMED YOUR EVERY MOVE,
WHAT DID THEY SEE?
THOSE FANS ARE NOW YOUR ENEMY.
NOW YOU HOLD OUT YOUR HAT.

ONE WRONG MOVE
AND YOU MAY NEVER GET BACK THE CROWD.
DON'T SHOW THE MIND BEHIND YOUR MASK.
IMPERFECT NOT ALLOWED.

PROUD ARE YOU,
IN TATTERS, YOU'RE STILL STANDING TALL,
ONE FALLEN STAR, WELL NOW YOU'LL PLAY
YOUR GREATEST ROLE OF ALL!

(*a knock on the door.* DAYTON *opens it.* JENNY *is there*)

JENNY
Are you alright, Miss Dayton?

DAYTON
Jenny, I had the strangest feeling just now…

JENNY
I did, too.

DAYTON
Please come in.

JENNY
I walked through those small-minded people out there, but it didn't bother me. Know why? Because you're a true actress, Miss Dayton. You believe in what you're doing.

DAYTON
You have to, dear. A movie worth fighting for is bound to offend someone. And if you can accept that, then maybe you can be an actress.

JENNY
Do you think so?

DAYTON
Please sit down, dear.
(JENNY *takes a seat*)
You have the talent. Both Joseph and I are impressed. Would you like anything, a soda?

JENNY
Oh, no, I'm just fine, thank you.

DAYTON
(*Standing by the chair, looking down*)
You are a godsend, Jenny.

JENNY
I have a secret to share, Miss Dayton. You see, I knew from the very first day when you arrived in Rosa Valley, that we would understand each other perfectly.

DAYTON
Isn't fate sometimes a gift? All you need are some friendly connections, and here's where maybe I can pay you back for being such an angel.

JENNY
Oh, you don't have to pay me back for anything, Miss Dayton.

DAYTON

But I want to, and I am…

(SHE *looks into* JENNY'S *eyes, smiling*)

…for something special that happened when I stepped off the train and saw your innocent young face beaming through the crowd. What memories it brings back…

SONG: "GOOD BYE, DEAR FAN"

GOOD BYE, DEAR FAN.
HELLO FRIEND!
WHEN THE CROWDS ARE GONE
I KNOW YOU'LL BE HERE.
YOU CAME TO ME WITH SUCH SWEET DEVOTION,
NOW I'M DEVOTED TO YOU.
MY WORLD IS YOURS IN RETURN.
SAY HELLO, DEAR FRIEND,
TO OUR GOOD FORTUNE.
FOLLOW YOUR DREAMS TO L.A.
AND I'LL MAKE THEM COME TRUE.

BREAKFAST BY A SUN KISSED SHORE…

(SHE *sits down beside* JENNY)

NIGHTS ON THE RUN, SUNSET BOULEVARD.
SAY YOU WANT THE SILVER SCREEN,
I'LL OPEN DOORS, IT WON'T BE HARD.
SO SPEND THE NIGHT IF YOU WISH.
YOU ARE HERE, IT'S LATE,
TOO LATE TO LEAVE NOW.
FATE MAY BE SMILING ON US —
LET TWO FRIENDS HAVE THEIR WAY.

(SHE *caresses* JENNY'S *shoulder lightly*)

SHARE THE MAGIC WITH ME.
ARE YOU THINKING YOU MIGHT STAY?

(DAYTON'S *subtle passes, born of loneliness, have made* JENNY *nervous, off balance in a relationship of fan worship. Turning the tables leaves her suddenly feeling strangely disconnected, and no longer in such thrall to* DAYTON, *who has started to give her a little hug, but then wisely pulls back*)

JENNY

Oh, that is so lovely of you! So generous and something...something wonderful to think about, Miss Dayton. Something to dream about! And it's getting late.

(SHE *rises*)

DAYTON

I understand. It's always getting late. And what's becoming of me. I only wish the best for you, Jenny.

JENNY

Oh, I'm flattered by your offer to help me. I really am. (*pause*) I have so many dreams, sometimes I feel crowded by them all.

DAYTON

(*rising, too, though reluctantly*)

I'm sorry.

(JENNY *drifts towards the door*)

How strange hearing myself say "I'm sorry."

JENNY

Oh, you don't have to be sorry for anything, Miss Dayton. You were so nice to let me visit you. I'll never forget.

(SHE *turns to continue on*)

DAYTON

And you were so sweet to come.

(JENNY *stands by the door, hesitant, not glancing back upon* DAYTON, *but to the side*)

An old studio chief once told me — "don't let a fan see you close up for more than two minutes — one minute in Europe — fifteen seconds in Paris, not only will they lose faith in you, but the entire industry suffers."

JENNY

(*turning around to face* DAYTON)

Oh, I've seen a lot more than two minutes, and I haven't lost any faith in you, Miss Dayton! In fact, I only respect you even more.

(THEY *exchange knowing looks, as if both understand the undercurrents of what has occurred*)

And believe me, I mean it.

DAYTON

(*as* JENNY *steps out through the door*)

I do believe you, Jenny. You see, there must be this misty curtain between us for it to work. Look for me when the lights go down and the screen comes alive.

JENNY

(*out the door, calling back*)

Oh, I will! I will! And, please, be as proud as you make us!

(DAYTON *closes the door, crosses to the window and looks down upon the street below. A knock on the door.* SHE *opens it to find towers there*)

TOWERS

Brenda, we're leaving town tomorrow morning on an early train.

DAYTON

Tomorrow?

TOWERS

Too much heat. I hear Chambers is organizing a big protest, paying shills to make a scene outside the library tomorrow. The police chief is on our side, but I don't want this town to suffer. All the exteriors are now in the can. We'll wrap the interiors next week at Warner. The trucks are leaving middle of the night. Just stay here. I'll come by in the morning around eight to pick you up.

DAYTON

All right.

TOWERS
Oh, I saw Jenny on the way up. It would not be good for her to know about this.

DAYTON
How could she?

TOWERS
(*pausing at the door*)
She may be smarter than we think.

(HE *exits*)

SONG: "FALLEN STAR"

DAYTON
FALLEN STAR,
NO ONE WILL SHARE THE DARK WITH YOU,
SO FACE IT LIKE THE LONELY DO,
ANOTHER NIGHT IS HERE.
LISTEN FOR A TELEPHONE THAT NEVER RINGS
OR BUY THE LIE SOME STRANGER BRINGS,
ANOTHER NIGHT IS NEAR.

LOVERS MEET DOWN ON THE STREET,
THE SUMMER IS THEIRS.
UP HERE I LIE IN REVERIE
WITH ALL MY FAILED AFFAIRS.

FALLEN STAR:
HERE'S TO YOUR DAYS BY LOVE PURSUED.
HERE'S TO YOUR GREAT INGRATITUDE.
ANOTHER NIGHT...ALONE.

(*Now it is stone quiet on the street.* DAYTON *lies down on the bed, with her clothes on, and turns out a small lamp into darkness again. A faint siren is heard in the distance*)

HEDDA HOPPER'S VOICE

Hedda Hopper to America! Rumors running rampant of early exit for Brenda Dayton film said to be in trouble. Dayton winning affection from die-hard fans despite rumored breakup with husband number four, endless bickering with her novice director, and a mounting civic protest against the film itself. We'll call it just another daring saga for the queen of mature, award-winning cinema. Once again, in our book, Brenda Dayton holds her own as the heartbeat of Hollywood!

ACT II, SCENE 5: Outside the Rosa Valley train station.

Friday, the following morning. CAST and CREW enter the station with luggage in hand. JENNY enters, rather timidly, shying away from others, taking a more secretive position at the edge of the action so as to remain as anonymous as SHE was in the beginning of the play. THRALL and ANDY enter, crossing to the station door.

THRALL

(*to the now familiar refrain of "Making Movies"*)

MAKING WESTERNS,
HALF THE TIME I PRAYED FOR PROTECTION.
GOD, IF I GET OUT OF THIS ALIVE,
I'LL BE FAITHFUL.

ANDY

But what about your heroic ride in Death Valley?

THRALL

(*stopping*)

Heroic? Oh, was shooting that a lulu. I fell off the stage coach and slid down a hillside with a loose wheel trailing me, lost my mustache. The director came running after me, fearing for my life, I thought. But, no, the first words out of his mouth: Where is the mustache?

ANDY

Do you get to shoot real guns?

THRALL

Not in the movies, Andy. It's all fake.

(*Focus shifts to* BILL, *entering.* HE *looks around and discovers* JENNY)

BILL

Jenny. There you are.

JENNY

(*with a big smile*)

Hi, Bill.

BILL
Did you get to talk to Mr. Towers about going to Hollywood?

JENNY
Oh, no. I didn't try. I gave it some serious thought, and I decided that sometimes it's better for a dream not to come true.

BILL
Yeah. (*pause*) After everything that went on here, I'm not so sure making movies would be the life for me.

JENNY
Besides, Bill, I don't think I could ever leave Rosa Valley.

BILL
We have our own palm trees.

(THEY *exchange warm smiles*)

My Dad said he'll help put me through college in civil engineering, and I can still minor in drama.

JENNY
That's wonderful, Bill. We have to be practical, don't we.

BILL
And I've decided, Jenny, I'm not going to accept a position at city hall if Mr. Chambers gets elected. I think he went too far against the movie, and that makes me nervous. There has to be a better way. I want to say good bye to Ted Thrall. Would you like to go with me?

JENNY
Oh, no, I'll stay right here, Bill. Please tell him good bye for me.

BILL

(*heading towards the station door*)

I will!

(DAYTON *enters, looks around, spots* JENNY, *starts to go in her direction, but holds off.* JENNY *notices her, and the two wave, but hold their distance, honoring that which makes* JENNY *the fan she still wants mostly to be*)

TOWERS

(*inadvertently diverting* DAYTON'S *focus off* JENNY)

Well, we did it.

DAYTON

Yes, we did, Sidney. I wonder how it will all come out?

TOWERS

I had a call from Rudy.

DAYTON

You did?

TOWERS

He said to give you his best. He will call you next week, and, can you keep a secret?

(DAYTON *gives him a look*)

He might be here to see you off. Look for his orange cap.

DAYTON

Oh, but I must see him!

TOWNERS

(*pushing her back, as a train whistle goes off*)

No, you mustn't. Calm down, for Rudy's sake. He'd be left behind to suffer. Besides, you'll miss your train.

DAYTON

No train leaves without me!

TOWERS

You are so hopelessly Hollywood!

ANDY

(*to* THRALL, *as* MRS. TOMS *comes rushing in*)

I want to be like James Dean.

MRS. TOMS

My, oh my.

ANDY
Whose your role model, mother?

MRS. TOMS
You'll never guess in a million years.

ANDY
Ma Kettle?
(A final train whistle, and an "All Aboard!")

THRALL
(calling out)
The world may pass you by. Brenda!

DAYTON
If it does, I'll find another one!

SONG: "MAKING MOVIES"
(slowly at first, gradually building)

MAKING MOVIES, SOMETIMES I GET LOST IN THE STORY.
ROSA VALLEY, STRANGE BUT TRUE,
THIS FEELS LIKE A BREAK UP,
KNOWING WHEN YOU'RE GONE, HOW I WILL MISS YOU.
KNOWING I MAY WAKE UP
RESTLESS AND BLUE.
YES, A STAR IS HUMAN TOO

IF I HAVE CAUSED YOU UNDUE PAIN,
FORGIVE ME, PLEASE, AND KNOW I WON'T FORGET
FEELING YOUR GOODNESS HERE ON THE SET

MAKING MOVES IS AN ART MY HEART IS A SLAVE TO.
THANK YOU, ROSA VALLEY, YOU WERE PART OF THE MAGIC
YOU WERE MORE THAN EXTRAS,
YOU WERE PEOPLE.
AND YOU MADE IT REAL...

CONDUCTOR'S VOICE
All aboard!

DAYTON
(*calling back*)
COMING, I AM!
(*rushing off to make the train, and then looking back*)
ROSA VALLEY,
AU REVOIR!

(*Sounds of the train chugging slowly off.* BILL *takes* JENNY'S *hand, and they wave. A man in an orange baseball cap enters, and eagerly gazes at the departing train. He sees the object of his being there, and waves, too, and a sudden smile on his face suggests that he and* DAYTON *have spotted each other.* HE *throws her a kiss*)

END OF MUSICAL

ABOUT THE AUTHOR

DAVID LEWIS grew up in a family of dreamers drawn to arts and amusements. Across the street loomed San Francisco's Playland at the Beach, where his father worked as an electrician, and one of his uncles managed the Big Dipper roller coaster. On his mother's side, a great uncle, Eugene B. Lewis, supervised 17 scenario writers at Universal during the silent era. And he scripted for such directors as John Ford.

Lewis presented touring puppet shows at grammar school, and was first published at the age of 14 in *The White Tops* magazine. He numbers among his most magical boyhood memories a fall evening in Santa Rosa outside the public library. There, he, his mother and sister had been hired as extras to appear in a crowd scene being filmed for the movie, *Storm Center.* After walking the grounds during a long exciting set up, he was transfixed by the fleeting images of make believe — Bette Davis in the near-darkness exchanging a few words with another actor while the cameras rolled, and pausing between takes, and then repeating the same scene all over again. How quickly had the magic passed.

He began writing musicals during his days at San Francisco State College. He co-wrote, produced and directed the annual student revue, *Kampus Kapers,* out of which came four cast members destined to reach Broadway stages, including Denny Martin Flinn and Kathryn Grody. One of *Kapers'* composers and its musical director, Shirley Walker, achieved fame in Hollywood as one of the first women to earn sole credit for a major motion picture score.

In Los Angeles, his musical *Those Ringlings,* with music by David Baron, rang up ringing notices ("Better than Barnum...Deserves a shot at the Tony" — *Variety*). Another of his works, *Calling in Sick,* won kudos for the Max Dancer score ("a legacy of music, entertain it does" — *Drama-Logue;* "show stopping" — *L.A. Weekly*)

Lewis is also the author of several acclaimed books on circus and theater, among them, *Big Top Boss: John Ringling North and the Circus; Inside the Changing Circus;* and *Broadway Musicals: A Hundred Year History.* From the latter, a chapter on Steven Sondheim was reprinted in Gale's Drama Criticism 2004. He is currently at work on a workplace memoir, *Keep That Day Job! How to Enjoy Chasing Showbiz in Vain.*

Red Cameras Roll was recently accepted by New York producer James Morgan for a workshop reading at his York Theatre.

www.ingramcontent.com/pod-product-compliance
Lightning Source LLC
LaVergne TN
LVHW010453160826
845677LV00012B/2464

9798887711492